poems 1965-1980

derek walcott

poems 1965-1980

JONATHAN CAPE

London

First published in this edition 1992
© Derek Walcott 1963, 1964, 1965, 1969,
1976, 1977, 1978, 1979
Jonathan Cape, 20 Vauxhall Bridge Road,
London, SW1V 2SA

A CIP catalogue record for this book
is available from the British Library

ISBN 0-224-03769-2

Printed in Great Britain by
Cox and Wyman Ltd, Reading

Acknowledgments

Some of these poems first appeared in the *London Magazine*, the *Spectator*, *The Times*, *Encounter*, the *Review of English Literature*, the *Chicago Tribune*, *New Letters*, *Co-operation*, the *Beliot Poetry Journal*, the *Borestone Mountain Poetry Awards 1963*, the *Bulletin*, *Art and Man*, *Bim*, *Caribbean Quarterly*, *Tapia* and the *Guyana Festival Anthology*, *Antaeus*. The poems entitled 'To Return to the Trees' and 'Sunday Lemons', 'The Bright Field' and 'Midsummer England' appeared originally in the *New Yorker*; © 1974, 1974, 1976, 1976, The New Yorker Magazine, Inc.

CONTENTS

The Gulf and other poems (1969)

Sea Grapes (1976)

The Star-Apple Kingdom (1980)

The Castaway
and other poems

The Castaway

The starved eye devours the seascape for the morsel
Of a sail.

The horizon threads it infinitely.

Action breeds frenzy. I lie,
Sailing the ribbed shadow of a palm,
Afraid lest my own footprints multiply.

Blowing sand, thin as smoke,
Bored, shifts its dunes.
The surf tires of its castles like a child.

The salt green vine with yellow trumpet-flower,
A net, inches across nothing.
Nothing: the rage with which the sandfly's head is filled.

Pleasures of an old man:
Morning: contemplative evacuation, considering
The dried leaf, nature's plan.

In the sun, the dog's faeces
Crusts, whitens like coral.
We end in earth, from earth began.
In our own entrails, genesis.

If I listen I can hear the polyp build,
The silence thwanged by two waves of the sea.
Cracking a sea-louse, I make thunder split.

Godlike, annihilating godhead, art
And self, I abandon
Dead metaphors: the almond's leaf-like heart,

The ripe brain rotting like a yellow nut
Hatching
Its babel of sea-lice, sandfly and maggot,

That green wine bottle's gospel choked with sand,
Labelled, a wrecked ship,
Clenched seawood nailed and white as a man's hand.

The Swamp

Gnawing the highway's edges, its black mouth
Hums quietly: 'Home, come home ...'

Behind its viscous breath the very word 'growth'
Grows fungi, rot;
White mottling its root.

More dreaded
Than canebrake, quarry, or sun-shocked gully-bed
Its horrors held Hemingway's hero rooted
To sure, clear shallows.

It begins nothing. Limbo of cracker convicts, Negroes.
Its black mood
Each sunset takes a smear of your life's blood.

Fearful, original sinuosities! Each mangrove sapling
Serpentlike, its roots obscene
As a six-fingered hand,

Conceals within its clutch the mossbacked toad,
Toadstools, the potent ginger-lily,
Petals of blood,

The speckled vulva of the tiger-orchid;
Outlandish phalloi
Haunting the travellers of its one road.

Deep, deeper than sleep
Like death,
Too rich in its decrescence, too close of breath,

In the fast-filling night, note
How the last bird drinks darkness with its throat,
How the wild saplings slip

Backward to darkness, go black
With widening amnesia, take the edge
Of nothing to them slowly, merge

Limb, tongue and sinew into a knot
Like chaos, like the road
Ahead.

Dogstar

The dogstar's rabid. Our street
burns its spilt garbage. Spent with heat
I brood on three good friends
dead in one year,
one summer's shock,
here where summer never ends.
I shall meet them there, I shall meet them there!

Beyond the window where I work
a neighbour's child
doubled in glass
seems to be walking among cloud,
below her feet
the flames of grass
are fuelled by their burning blood.
The dog, the dog will have its meat!

Sweat-drenched, muttering aloud,
I see a childhood uncle, mad, now dead,
sweating to whittle a cane stalk, a bead
jewels his forehead like the toad.
I cannot put day's burning smell aside
like a new book I am too tired to read.

Shovelled in like sticks to feed earth's raging oven,
consumed like heretics in this poem's pride,
these clouds, their white smoke, make and unmake heaven.

The Flock

The grip of winter tightening, its thinned
volleys of blue-wing teal and mallard fly
from the longbows of reeds bent by the wind,
arrows of yearning for our different sky.
A season's revolution hones their sense,
whose target is our tropic light, while I
awoke this sunrise to a violence
of images migrating from the mind.
Skeletal forest, a sepulchral knight
riding in silence at a black tarn's edge
hooves cannonading snow
in the white funeral of the year,
antlike across the forehead of an alp
in iron contradiction crouched
against those gusts that urge the mallards south.
Vizor'd with blind defiance of his quest,
its yearly divination of the spring.
I travel through such silence, making dark
symbols with this pen's print across snow,
measuring winter's augury by words
settling the branched mind like migrating birds,
and never question when they come or go.

The style, tension of motion and the dark,
inflexible direction of the world
as it revolves upon its centuries
with change of language, climate, customs, light,
with our own prepossession day by day

year after year with images of flight,
survive our condemnation and the sun's
exultant larks.
        The dark, impartial Arctic
whose glaciers encased the mastodon,
froze giant minds in marble attitudes
revolves with tireless, determined grace
upon an iron axle, though the seals
howl with inhuman cries across its ice
and pages of torn birds are blown across
whitening tundras like engulfing snow.

Till its annihilation may the mind
reflect his fixity through winter, tropic,
until that equinox when the clear eye
clouds, like a mirror, without contradiction,
greet the black wings that cross it as a blessing
like the high, whirring flock that flew across
the cold sky of this page when I began
this journey by the wintry flare of dawn,
flying by instinct to their secret places
both for their need and for my sense of season.

A Village Life

(for John Robertson)

I

Through the wide, grey loft window,
I watched that winter morning, my first snow
crusting the sill, puzzle the black,
nuzzling tom. Behind my back
a rime of crud glazed my cracked coffee-cup,
a snowfall of torn poems piling up
heaped by a rhyming spade.
Starved, on the prowl,
I was a frightened cat in that grey city.
I floated, a cat's shadow, through the black wool
sweaters, leotards and parkas of the fire-haired,
snow-shouldered Greenwich Village mädchen,
homesick, my desire
crawled across snow
like smoke, for its lost fire.

All that winter I haunted
your house on Hudson Street, a tiring friend,
demanding to be taken in, drunk, and fed.
I thought winter would never end.

I cannot imagine you dead.

But that stare, frozen,
a frosted pane in sunlight,
gives nothing back by letting nothing in,
your kindness or my pity.

No self-reflection lies
within those silent, ice-blue irises,
whose image is some snow-locked mountain lake
in numb Montana.

And since that winter I have learnt to gaze
on life indifferently as through a pane of glass.

II

Your image rattled on the subway glass
is my own death-mask in an overcoat;
under New York, the subterranean freight
of human souls, locked in an iron cell,
station to station cowed with swaying calm,
thunders to its end, each in its private hell,
each plumped, prime bulk still swinging by its arm
upon a hook. You're two years dead. And yet
I watch that silence spreading through our souls:
that horn-rimmed midget who consoles
his own deformity with Sartre on Genet.
Terror still eats the nerves, the Word
is gibberish, the plot Absurd.
The turnstile slots, like addicts, still consume
obols and aspirin, Charon in his grilled cell
grows vague about our crime, our destination.
Not all are silent, or endure
the enormity of silence; at one station,
somewhere off 33rd and Lexington,
a fur-wrapped matron screamed above the roar
of rattling iron. Nobody took her on,
We looked away. Such scenes
rattle our trust in nerves tuned like machines.
All drives as you remember it, the pace
of walking, running the rat race,
locked in a system, ridden by its rail,
within a life where no one dares to fail.
I watch your smile breaking across my skull,
the hollows of your face below my face

sliding across it like a pane of glass.
Nothing endures. Even in his cities
man's life is grass.
Times Square. We sigh and let off steam,
who should screech with the braking wheels, scream
like our subway-Cassandra, heaven-sent
to howl for Troy, emerge
blind from the blast of daylight, whirled
apart like papers from a vent.

III

Going away, through Queen's we pass
a cemetery of miniature skyscrapers. The verge
blazes its rust, its taxi-yellow leaves. It's fall.
I stare through glass,
my own reflection there, at
empty avenues, lawns, spires, quiet
stones, where the curb's rim
wheels westward, westward, where thy bones ...

Montana, Minnesota, your real
America, lost in tall grass, serene idyll.

A Tropical Bestiary

IBIS

Flare of the ibis, rare vermilion,
A hieroglyphic of beak-headed Egypt
That haunts, they claim, the green swamp-traveller
Who catches it to watch its plumage fade,
Loses its colours in captivity,
Blanches into a pinkish, stilted heron
Among the garrulous fishwife gulls, bitterns and spoonbills
And ashen herons of the heronry.
She never pines, complains at being kept,
Yet, imperceptibly, fades from her fire,
Pointing no moral but the fact
Of flesh that has lost pleasure in the act,
Of domesticity, drained of desire.

OCTOPUS

Post coitum, omne animal ... from love
The eight limbs loosen, like tentacles in water,
Like the slow tendrils of
The octopus.
                    Fathoms down
They drift, numbed by the shock
Of an electric charge, drown
Vague as lidless fishes, separate
Like the anemone from rock
The sleek eel from its sea-cleft, drawn
By the darkening talons of the tide.
Pulse of the sea in the locked, heaving side.

LIZARD

Fear:
        the heraldic lizard, magnified,
Devouring its midge.
            Last night I plucked
'as a brand from the burning', a murderous, pincered beetle
Floundering in urine like a shipwreck shallop
Rudderless, its legs frantic as oars.
Did I, by this act, set things right side up?
It was not death I dreaded but the fight
With nothing. The aged, flailing their claws
On flowery coverlets, may dread such salvation,
The impotence of rescue or compassion.
Rightening a beetle damns creation.
It may have felt more terror on its back
When my delivering fingers, huge as hell,
Shadowed the stiffening victim with their jaws
Than the brown lizard, Galapagos-large,
Waggling its horny tail at morning's morsel
Held for the midge.
            Mercy has strange laws.
Withdraw and leave the scheme of things in charge.

MAN O' WAR BIRD

The idling pivot of the frigate bird
Sways the world's scales, tilts cobalt sea and sky,
Rightens, by its round eye, my drift
Through heaven when I shift
My study of the sun.
            The easy wings
Depend upon the stress I give such things
As my importance to its piercing height, the peace
Of its slow, ravening circuit of a speck
Upon a beach prey to its beak
Like any predatory tern it seizes.
In that blue wildfire somewhere is an Eye
That weighs this world exactly as it pleases.

SEA CRAB

The sea crab's cunning, halting, awkward grace
is the syntactical envy of my hand;
obliquity burrowing to surface
from hot, plain sand.
Those who require vision, complexity,
tire of its distressing
limits: sea, sand, scorching sky.
Cling to this ground, though constellations race,
the horizon burn, the wave coil, hissing,
salt sting the eye.

THE WHALE, HIS BULWARK

To praise the blue whale's crystal jet,
To write, 'O fountain!' honouring a spout
Provokes this curse:
        'The high are humbled yet'
From those who humble Godhead, beasthood, verse.

Once, the Lord raised this bulwark to our eyes,
Once, in our seas, whales threshed,
The harpooner was common. Once, I heard
Of a baleine beached up the Grenadines, fleshed
By derisive, antlike villagers: a prize
Reduced from majesty to pygmy-size.
Salt-crusted, mythological,
And dead.

The boy who told me couldn't believe his eyes,
And I believed him. When I was small
God and a foundered whale were possible.
Whales are rarer, God as invisible.
Yet, through His gift, I praise the unfathomable,
Though the boy may be dead, the praise unfashionable,
The tale apocryphal.

TARPON

At Cedros, thudding the dead sand
in spasms, the tarpon
gaped with a gold eye, drowned
thickly, thrashing with brute pain
this sea I breathe.
Stilled, its bulk,
screwed to the eye's lens, slowly
sought design. It dried like silk,
leisurely, altered to lead.
The belly, leprous, silver, bulged
like a cold chancre for the blade.
Suddenly it shuddered in immense
doubt, but the old jaw, gibbering, divulged
nothing but some new filaments
of blood. For every bloody stroke
with which a frenzied fisherman struck
its head my young son shook his head.
Could I have called out not to look
simply at the one world we shared?
Dead, and examined in detail,
a tarpon's bulk grows beautiful.

Bronze, with a brass-green mould, the scales
age like a corselet of coins,
a net of tarnished silver joins
the back's deep-sea blue to the tail's
wedged, tapering Y.
Set in a stone, triangular skull,
ringing with gold, the open eye
is simply, tiringly there.
A shape so simple, like a cross,
a child could draw it in the air.
A tarpon's scale, its skin's flake
washed at the sea's edge and held
against the light looks just like what
the grinning fisherman said it would:
dense as frost glass but delicate,

etched by a diamond, it showed
a child's drawing of a ship,
the sails' twin triangles, a mast.

Can such complexity of shape,
such bulk, terror and fury fit
in a design so innocent,
that through opaque, phantasmal mist,
moving, but motionlessly, it
sails where imagination sent?

Missing The Sea

Something removed roars in the ears of this house,
Hangs its drapes windless, stuns mirrors
Till reflections lack substance.

Some sound like the gnashing of windmills ground
To a dead halt;
A deafening absence, a blow.

It hoops this valley, weighs this mountain,
Estranges gesture, pushes this pencil
Through a thick nothing now,

Freights cupboards with silence, folds sour laundry
Like the clothes of the dead left exactly
As the dead behaved by the beloved,

Incredulous, expecting occupancy.

The Glory Trumpeter

Old Eddie's face, wrinkled with river lights,
Looked like a Mississippi man's. The eyes,
Derisive and avuncular at once,
Swivelling, fixed me. They'd seen
Too many wakes, too many cat-house nights.
The bony, idle fingers on the valves
Of his knee-cradled horn could tear
Through 'Georgia On My Mind' or 'Jesus Saves'
With the same fury of indifference
If what propelled such frenzy was despair.

Now, as the eyes sealed in the ashen flesh,
And Eddie, like a deacon at his prayer,
Rose, tilting the bright horn, I saw a flash
Of gulls and pigeons from the dunes of coal
Near my grandmother's barracks on the wharves,
I saw the sallow faces of those men
Who sighed as if they spoke into their graves
About the negro in America. That was when
The Sunday comics, sprawled out on her floor,
Sent from the States, had a particular odour;
Dry smell of money mingled with man's sweat.

And yet, if Eddie's features held our fate,
Secure in childhood I did not know then
A jesus-ragtime or gut-bucket blues
To the bowed heads of lean, compliant men
Back from the States in their funereal serge

Black, rusty Homburgs and limp waiters' ties,
Slow, honey accents and lard-coloured eyes
Was Joshua's ram's horn wailing for the Jews
Of patient bitterness or bitter seige.

Now it was that, as Eddie turned his back
On our young crowd out fêteing, swilling liquor,
And blew, eyes closed, one foot up, out to sea,
His horn aimed at those cities of the Gulf,
Mobile and Galveston, and sweetly meted
Their horn of plenty through his bitter cup,
In lonely exaltation blaming me
For all whom race and exile have defeated,
For my own uncle in America,
That living there I never could look up.

Goats and Monkeys

... even now, an old black ram
is tupping your white ewe.
Othello

The owl's torches gutter. Chaos clouds the globe.
Shriek, augury! His earthen bulk
buries her bosom in its slow eclipse.
His smoky hand has charred
that marble throat. Bent to her lips,
he is Africa, a vast, sidling shadow
that halves your world with doubt.
'Put out the light', and God's light is put out.

That flame extinct, she contemplates her dream
of him as huge as night, as bodiless,
as starred with medals, like the moon
a fable of blind stone.
Dazzled by that bull's bulk against the sun
of Cyprus, couldn't she have known
like Pasiphaë, poor girl, she'd breed horned monsters?
That like Euyridice, her flesh a flare
travelling the hellish labyrinth of his mind
his soul would swallow hers?

Her white flesh rhymes with night. She climbs, secure.

Virgin and ape, maid and malevolent Moor,
their immoral coupling still halves our world.
He is your sacrificial beast, bellowing, goaded,
a black bull snarled in ribbons of its blood.
And yet, whatever fury girded
on that saffron-sunset turban, moon-shaped sword

was not his racial, panther-black revenge
pulsing her chamber with raw musk, its sweat,
but horror of the moon's change,
of the corruption of an absolute,
like a white fruit
pulped ripe by fondling but doubly sweet.

And so he barbarously arraigns the moon
for all she has beheld since time began
for his own night-long lechery, ambition,
while barren innocence whimpers for pardon.

And it is still the moon, she silvers love,
limns lechery and stares at our disgrace.
Only annihilation can resolve
the pure corruption in her dreaming face.

A bestial, comic agony. We harden
with mockery at this blackamoor
who turns his back on her, who kills
what, like the clear moon, cannot abhor
her element, night; his grief
farcically knotted in a handkerchief
a sibyl's
prophetically stitched remembrancer
webbed and embroidered with the zodiac,
this mythical, horned beast who's no more
monstrous for being black.

The Prince

Genderers of furies, crouching, slavering beasts
those paps that gave me suck! His dragonish scales
are velvet-sheathed, even at those feasts
of coiling tongues. Lust has not soured
that milky stomach. Something more than love
my father lacked which God will not approve:

a savage, sundering sword, vile to the touch
breeding fidelity by its debauch.
Calm, she reclines on her maternal couch,
knitting revenge and lechery in my head.
I ease the sword, and, like her victim, quaking,
I, in my father, stalk my father's dread.

The Wedding of an Actress

Entering from the glare
Of the mid-morning traffic, we assume
Our lily-bordered pew; our eyes
Gradually grow familiar with the gloom.
I recognize that dais
Branching with candles as the stage, the smiles
Exchanged between the carved and living face,
That altar tapestry's archaic zeal
Of harvest, and at the crowd's
Slow scything at the knee, I kneel.

Knowing I am a guest in the Lord's house,
I seal my sense in darkness to admit
That moment where irreconcilables knit
'in a white rose, shaped from the soldiery
which, with His own blood, Christ hath made His spouse.
I press my forehead hard on the scarred pews,
Wrestle with prayer and fail.
It is no use.
In any church my brain is a charred vault
Where demons roost,
A blackened, shifting dust.

A kyrie shrills, hysterical as the ghost
Of a dead marriage in the ear. Nothing is real,
Through my own fault, through my most grievous fault.

And nothing swarms the sight
Until the choir, altering its mood,
Proclaims the bride. The bride. To its diapason,
Between banked lilies and the hallowed stone,
A crystal of calm blood,
Sails her veiled body evenly as the swan,
White as Ophelia on the black flood.

II

We too are actors, who behold
This ceremony; we hold
Our breath, defying dissolution,
Faith, we were told, like art,
Feeds on illusion.

III

Through the illusion of another life,
I can observe this custom like a ghost,
Watching the incense snaking overhead
Dissolving like the wafer laid
In wine along the tongue,
Hearing their promise buried in this vault,
Their lines drowned in the surges of a song.
Yet whether faith or custom matters most,
In each the private tragedy is lost.
Faith is as virginal as every bride,
Custom the church from which I am divorced
Because of pride, because of grievous pride.

Laventville

(for V. S. Naipaul)

To find the Western Path
Through the Gates of Wrath
Blake

It huddled there
steel tinkling its blue painted metal air,
tempered in violence, like Rio's favelas,

with snaking, perilous streets whose edges fell as
its episcopal turkey-buzzards fall
from its miraculous hilltop

shrine,
down the impossible drop
to Belmont, Woodbrook, Maraval, St Clair

that shine
like peddlers' tin trinkets in the sun.
From a harsh

shower, its gutters growled and gargled wash
past the Youth Centre, past the water catchment,
a rigid children's carousel of cement;

we climbed where lank electric
lines and tension cables linked its raw brick
hovels like a complex feud,

where the inheritors of the middle passage stewed
five to a room, still clamped below their hatch,
breeding like felonies,

whose lives revolve round prison, graveyard, church.
Below bent breadfruit trees
in the flat, coloured city, class

lay escalated into structures still,
merchant, middleman, magistrate, knight. To go downhill
from here was to ascend.

The middle passage never guessed its end.
This is the height of poverty
for the desperate and black;

climbing, we could look back
with widening memory
on the hot, corrugated iron sea
whose horrors we all

shared. The salt blood knew it well,
you, me, Samuel's daughter, Samuel,
and those ancestors clamped below its grate.

And climbing steeply past the wild
gutters, it shrilled
in the blood, for those who suffered, who were killed,

and who survive.
What other gift was there to give
as the godparents of his unnamed child?

Yet outside the brown annexe of the church, the
stifling odour of bay rum and talc, the particular,
neat sweetness of the crowd distressed

that sense. The black, fawning verger
his bow tie akimbo, grinning, the clown-gloved
fashionable wear of those I deeply loved

once, made me look on with hopelessness and rage
at their new, apish habits, their excess
and fear, the possessed, the self-possessed;

their perfume shrivelled to a childhood fear
of Sabbath graveyards, christenings, marriages,
that muggy, steaming, self-assuring air

of tropical Sabbath afternoons. And in
the church, eyes prickling with rage,
the children rescued from original sin

by their God-father since the middle passage,
the supercilious brown curate, who intones,

healing the guilt in these rachitic bones,
twisting my love within me like a knife,
'across the troubled waters of this life ... '

Which of us cares to walk
even if God wished
those retching waters where our souls were fished

for this new world? Afterwards, we talk
in whispers, close to death
among these stones planted on alien earth.

Afterwards,
the ceremony, the careful photograph
moved out of range before the patient tombs,

we dare a laugh,
ritual, desperate words,
born like these children from habitual wombs,

from lives fixed in the unalterable groove
of grinding poverty. I stand out on a balcony
and watch the sun pave its flat, golden path

across the roofs, the aerials, cranes, the tops
of fruit trees crawling downward to the city.
Something inside is laid wide like a wound,

some open passage that has cleft the brain,
some deep, amnesiac blow. We left
somewhere a life we never found,

customs and gods that are not born again,
some crib, some grill of light
clanged shut on us in bondage, and withheld

us from that world below us and beyond,
and in its swaddling cerements we're still bound.

The Almond Trees

There's nothing here
this early;
cold sand
cold churning ocean, the Atlantic,
no visible history,

except this stand
of twisted, coppery, sea-almond trees
their shining postures surely
bent as metal, and one

foam-haired, salt-grizzled fisherman,
his mongrel growling, whirling on the stick
he pitches him; its spinning rays
'no visible history'
until their lengthened shapes amaze the sun.

By noon,
this further shore of Africa is strewn
with the forked limbs of girls toasting their flesh
in scarves, sunglasses, Pompeian bikinis,

brown daphnes, laurels, they'll all have
like their originals, their sacred grove,
this frieze
of twisted, coppery, sea-almond trees.

The fierce acetylene air
has singed
their writhing trunks with rust, the same
hues as a foundered, peeling barge.
It'll sear a pale skin copper with its flame.

The sand's white-hot ash underheel,
but their aged limbs have got their brazen sheen
from fire. Their bodies fiercely shine!
They're cured,
they endured their furnace.

Aged trees and oiled limbs share a common colour!

Welded in one flame,
huddling naked, stripped of their name,
for Greek or Roman tags, they were lashed
raw by wind, washed
out with salt and fire-dried,
bitterly nourished where their branches died,

their leaves' broad dialect a coarse,
enduring sound
they shared together.

Not as some running hamadryad's cries
rooted, broke slowly into leaf
her nipples peaking to smooth, wooden boles

Their grief
howls seaward through charred, ravaged holes.

One sunburnt body now acknowledges
that past and its own metamorphosis
as, moving from the sun, she kneels to spread
her wrap within the bent arms of this grove
that grieves in silence, like parental love.

Veranda

(for Ronald Bryden)

Grey apparitions at veranda ends
like smoke, divisible, but one
your age is ashes, its coherence gone,

Planters whose tears were marketable gum, whose voices
scratch the twilight like dried fronds
edged with reflection,

Colonels, hard as the commonwealth's greenheart,
middlemen, usurers whose art
kept an empire in the red,

Upholders of Victoria's china seas
lapping embossed around a drinking mug,
bully-boy roarers of the Empire club,

To the tarantara of the bugler, the sunset furled
round the last post,
the 'flamingo colours' of a fading world,

A ghost steps from you, my grandfather's ghost!
Uprooted from some rainy English shire,
you sought your Roman

End in suicide by fire.
Your mixed son gathered your charred, blackened bones,
in a child's coffin.

And buried them himself on a strange coast.
Sire,
why do I raise you up? Because

Your house has voices, your burnt house,
shrills with unguessed, lovely inheritors,
your genealogical roof tree, fallen, survives,
like seasoned timber through green, little lives.

I ripen towards your twilight, sir, that dream
where I am singed in that sea-crossing, steam
towards that vaporous world, whose souls,

like pressured trees brought diamonds out of coals.
The sparks pitched from your burning house are stars.
I am the man my father loved and was.

Whatever love you suffered makes amends
within them, father.
I climb the stair

And stretch a darkening hand to greet those friends
who share with you the last inheritance
of earth, our shrine and pardoner,

grey, ghostly loungers at veranda ends.

Statues

Stone will not bleed;
Nor shall this vizor'd prince, apotheosized
On his stone steed,
A barrel-bellied charger treading air,
Its tightening haunches set
To hurdle with its warrior the chasm
Between our age and theirs.
Its eyes erupt, bulge in a spasm
Of marble. We stare
At their slow power to corrupt;

Then turn to read
Around another statue, civic-sized,
Bare, balding head,
Of some archaic, muscular aphorist
Laurelled, toga unkempt,
His forked hand raised like a diviner's rod,
His face creased with the wise
Exhaustion of a god.
Their eyes
Withhold amusement, mine, contempt.

Boys will be boys.
Who can instruct them where true honour lies?
Instinct or choice,
Proclaims it lies within
War's furious, dandiacal discipline.
We, who have known

Its victims huddled in a reeking ditch,
Of the shaft's iron light hurtling Saul
Into pedestrian sainthood at his fall,
Still praise that murderous energy of stone.

On them, your fatherly, exhausted air
Is lost,
As sightless as the god's prophetic stare.

Across that gulf each greets the other's ghost.

A Map of Europe

Like Leonardo's idea
Where landscapes open on a waterdrop
Or dragons crouch in stains,
My flaking wall, in the bright air,
Maps Europe with its veins.

On its limned window ledge
A beer can's gilded rim gleams like
Evening along a Canaletto lake,
Or like that rocky hermitage
Where, in his cell of light, haggard Jerome
Prays that His kingdom come
To the far city.

The light creates its stillness. In its ring
Everything IS. A cracked coffee cup,
A broken loaf, a dented urn become
Themselves, as in Chardin,
Or in beer-bright Vermeer,
Not objects of our pity.

In it is no lacrimae rerum,
No art. Only the gift
To see things as they are, halved by a darkness
From which they cannot shift.

Nights in the Gardens of Port of Spain

Night, our black summer, simplifies her smells
into a village; she assumes the impenetrable

musk of the Negro, grows secret as sweat,
her alleys odorous with shucked oyster shells,

coals of gold oranges, braziers of melon.
Commerce and tambourines increase her heat.

Hellfire or the whorehouse: crossing Park Street,
a surf of sailors' faces crests, is gone

with the sea's phosphorescence; the boîtes de nuit
twinkle like fireflies in her thick hair.

Blinded by headlamps, deaf to taxi klaxons,
she lifts her face from the cheap, pitch-oil flare

towards white stars, like cities, flashing neon,
burning to be the bitch she will become.

As daylight breaks the Indian turns his tumbril
of hacked, beheaded coconuts towards home.

God Rest Ye Merry Gentlemen

Splitting from Jack Delaney's, Sheridan Square,
that winter night, stewed, seasoned in bourbon,
my body kindled by the whistling air
snowing the Village that Christ was reborn,
I lurched like any lush by his own glow
across towards Sixth, and froze before the tracks
of footprints bleeding on the virgin snow.
I tracked them where they led across the street
to the bright side, entering the wax-
sealed smell of neon, human heat,
some all-night diner with its wise-guy cook
his stub thumb in my bowl of stew and one
man's pulped and beaten face, its look
acknowledging all that, white-dark outside,
was possible: some beast prowling the block,
something fur-clotted, running wild
beyond the boundary of will. Outside,
more snow had fallen. My heart charred.
I longed for darkness, evil that was warm.
Walking, I'd stop and turn. What had I heard,
wheezing behind my heel with whitening breath?
Nothing. Sixth Avenue yawned wet and wide.
The night was white. There was nowhere to hide.

November Sun

In our treacherous
seasonless climate's
dry heat or muggy heat or rain
I'm measuring winter by this November sun's
diagonals shafting the window pane,
by my crouched shadow's
embryo on the morning study-floor. Once

I wallowed in ignorance
of change, of windfall, snowfall,
skull-cracking heat, sea-threshing hurricane.
Now I'd prefer to know.
We age desiring
these icy intuitions
that seasons bring.

Look, they'll be pierced with knowledge
as with light! One boy, nine years in age
who vaults and tumbles, squirrelling
in his perpetual spring,
that ten-month, cautious totterer
my daughter.
I rarely let them in.

This is a sort of
death cell
where knowledge of our fatality is hidden.
I trace here, like a bent astronomer

the circle of the year,
nurturing its inner seasons'
mulch, drench, fire, ash.
In my son's
restless gaze
I am time-ridden,
the sedentary dial of his days.
Our shadows point one way,
even their brief shadows on the cropped morning grass.

I am pierced with this. I cannot look away.
Ah Christ, how cruelly the needles race!

'O Trees of Life, What are Your Signs of Winter?'

(for E.S.)

Her passion was for objects, the sane life
Displayed like crystal on blond oak,
Bowls, spatulas, snowy linen.
So, suddenly, when he died,
She wanted this blue vase
They'd seen in a show-window.
When I brought it, she said,
Her vision glazed with shock:
'Place this on a ledge
in winter, it irradiates Stockholm.'
Distracted? Our knowledge
Revolves in a blue sphere.
Passionate of breath
We cloud a little dome.

So I imagine her
This winter at a window,
Shawled, in an empty room
With two forgetting children,
In the blue globe I brought
Her when he died, her thought
Whirled rootlessly like snow.

Lines in New England

'The cruel lie of caste refute,
Old forms remould, and substitute
For Slavery's lash the freeman's will,
For blind routine, wise-handed skill;
A school-house plant on every hill,
Stretching in radiate nerve-lines thence
The quick wires of intelligence;
Till North and South together brought
Shall own the same electric thought,
In peace a common flag salute,
And, side by side in labour's free
And unresentful rivalry,
Harvest the fields wherein they fought!'–Whither: Snowbound

Geese creaking south, a raucous
chain unlocking winter's cavernous
barn, cross me
going the other way.
Why am I so far north,
who dread these stripped trees' polar
iron, and fear fall,
cinders and brimstone of
the pilgrim's prophecy? I look
from arrowing train lines at the track
this crabbed hand makes, at every trick
of its shot trade. It runs, cramped
from itself with loathing: the pumped
detonation under sulphurous

sheets, the white, treacherous
hands it has been gripped by;
a crab wallowing in the water of
a salt, warm, drifting eye;
the breasts it's held in love,
in hollow love. The ruled lie
it follows. Yet not once has this hand
sought to strike home. Outside,
an Indian summer whose trees radiate
like veins, a salt-blue pond,
where I imagine a crazed, single, deer-
skinned quarry drinking, the last
Mohican. Redcoat, redman, their thirst-
ing, autumn battle-ground,
its savage lacerations healed
by salt white spire and green field.
I watch from my side of the glass
the lantern slides clicking across
the window glazed by ocean air.
Mine, or another history there?
A civilization with its dreams
of guilt; the trails drive grittily,
their power clamps the jaw
tight with abhorrence and with love
these parallels, that seem to move
to blue infinity, laid down the law
of separate but equal love.

The Voyage Up River

(for Wilson Harris)

They roll as deaf as logs through foliage swollen
With elephantiasis to the green screech of macaws;

This is their second death, and they have fallen
All over, overboard, swirling like oars.

Does the piranha shred their bones of flesh
Again, boiled in the tide-race,

And the scaled cayman heave its hulk and flash
To halve their limbs in the original place?

On that vague expedition did their souls
Spawn, vaporous as butterflies, in resurrection,

Or the small terrors multiply like tadpoles
Below a mangrove root or a headstone?

Stillborn in death, their memory is not ours,
In whom the spasm of birth

Gendered oblivion. To chart empty savannahs,
Rivers, even with a guide, conceives an earth

Without us, without gods: Guiana or Guinea,
An aboriginal fear, lie Orinoco

Disgorging from a mouth brown with tobacco
Deaths that cannot discolour the great sea.

Crusoe's Journal

I looked now upon the world as a thing remote, which I had nothing
to do with, no expectation from, and, indeed no desires about. In a
word, I had nothing indeed to do with it, nor was ever like to have;
so I thought it looked as we may perhaps look upon it hereafter, viz.,
as a place I had lived in but was come out of it; and well might I say,
as Father Abraham to Dives, 'Between me and thee is a great gulf fixed.'

Robinson Crusoe

Once we have driven past Mundo Nuevo trace
          safely to this beach house
perched between ocean and green, churning forest
          the intellect appraises
objects surely, even the bare necessities
          of style are turned to use,
like those plain iron tools he salvages
          from shipwreck, hewing a prose
as odorous as raw wood to the adze,
          out of such timbers
came our first book, our profane Genesis
          whose Adam speaks that prose
which, blessing some sea-rock, startles itself
          with poetry's surprise,
in a green world, one without metaphors;
          like Christofer he bears
in speech mnemonic as a missionary's
          the Word to savages,
its shape an earthen, water-bearing vessel's
          whose sprinkling alters us
into good Fridays who recite His praise,
          parroting our master's
style and voice, we make his language ours,
          converted cannibals
we learn with him to eat the flesh of Christ.

All shapes, all objects multiplied from his,
          our ocean's Proteus;

in childhood, his derelict's old age
            was like a god's. (Now pass
in memory, in serene parenthesis,
            the cliff-deep leeward coast
of my own island filing past the noise
            of stuttering canvas,
some noon-struck village, Choiseul, Canaries,
            with crocodile canoes,
a savage settlement from Henty's novels,
            Marryat or R.L.S.,
with one boy signalling at the sea's edge,
            though what he cried is lost;)
So time that makes us objects, multiplies
            our natural loneliness.

For the hermetic skill, that from earth's clays
            shapes something without use,
and separate from itself, lives somewhere else,
            sharing with every beach
a longing for those gulls that cloud the cays
            with raw, mimetic cries,
never surrenders wholly for it knows
            it needs another's praise
like hoar, half-cracked Ben Gunn, until it cries
            at last, 'O happy desert!'
and learns again the self-creating peace
            of islands. So from this house
that faces nothing but the sea, his journals
            assume a household use,
We learn to shape from them, where nothing was
            the language of a race,
and since the intellect demands its mask
            that sun-cracked, bearded face
provides us with the wish to dramatize
            ourselves at nature's cost,
to attempt a beard, to squint through the sea-haze,
            posing as naturalists,

drunks, castaways, beachcombers, all of us
  yearn for those fantasies
of innocence, for our faith's arrested phase
  when the clear voice
startled itself saying 'water, heaven, Christ,'
  hoarding such heresies as
God's loneliness moves in His smallest creatures.

Crusoe's Island

I

The chapel's cowbell
Like God's anvil
Hammers ocean to a blinding shield;
Fired, the sea-grapes slowly yield
Bronze plates to the metallic heat.

Red, corrugated iron
Roofs roar in the sun.
The wiry, ribbed air
Above earth's open kiln
Writhes like a child's vision
Of hell, but nearer, nearer.

Below, the picnic plaid
Of Scarborough is spread
To a blue, perfect sky,
Dome of our hedonist philosophy.
Bethel and Canaan's heart
Lie open like a psalm.
I labour at my art.
My father, God, is dead.

Past thirty now I know
To love the self is dread
Of being swallowed by the blue
Of heaven overhead
Or rougher blue below.
Some lesion of the brain

From art or alcohol
Flashes this fear by day:
As startling as his shadow
Grows to the castaway.

Upon this rock the bearded hermit built
His Eden:
Goats, corn-crop, fort, parasol, garden,
Bible for sabbath, all the joys
But one
Which sent him howling for a human voice.
Exiled by a flaming sun
The rotting nut, bowled in the surf
Became his own brain rotting from the guilt
Of heaven without his kind,
Crazed by such paradisal calm
The spinal shadow of a palm
Built keel and gunwale in his mind.

The second Adam since the fall
His germinal
Corruption held the seed
Of that congenital heresy that men fail
According to their creed.
Craftsman and castaway
All heaven in his head,
He watched his shadow pray
Not for God's love but human love instead.

II

We came here for the cure
Of quiet in the whelk's centre,
From the fierce, sudden quarrel,
From kitchens where the mind
Like bread, disintegrates in water,
To let a salt sun scour
The brain as harsh as coral
To bathe like stones in wind,
To be, like beast or natural object, pure.

49

That fabled, occupational
Compassion, supposedly inherited with the gift
Of poetry had fed
With a rat's thrift on faith, shifted
Its trust to corners, hoarded
Its mania like bread,
Its brain a white, nocturnal bloom
That in a drunken, moonlit room
Saw my son's head
Swaddled in sheets
Like a lopped nut, lolling in foam.

O love, we die alone!
I am borne by the bell
Backward to boyhood
To the grey wood
Spire, harvest and marigold,
To those whom a cruel
Just God could gather
To His blue breast, His beard
A folding cloud,
As He gathered my father.
Irresolute and proud,
I can never go back.

I have lost sight of hell,
Of heaven, of human will,
My skill
Is not enough,
I am struck by this bell
To the root.
Crazed by a racking sun,
I stand at my life's noon,
On parched, delirious sand
My shadow lengthens.

III

Art is profane and pagan,

The most it has revealed
Is what a crippled Vulcan
Beat on Achilles' shield.
By these blue, changing graves
Fanned by the furnace blast
Of heaven, may the mind
Catch fire till it cleaves
Its mould of clay at last.

Now Friday's progeny,
The brood of Crusoe's slave,
Black little girls in pink
Organdy, crinolines,
Walk in their air of glory
Beside a breaking wave;
Below their feet the surf
Hisses like tambourines.

At dusk when they return
For vespers, every dress
Touched by the sun will burn
A seraph's, an angel's,
And nothing I can learn
From art or loneliness
Can bless them as the bell's
Transfiguring tongue can bless.

Lampfall

Closest at lampfall
Like children, like the moth-flame metaphor,
The Coleman's humming jet at the sea's edge
A tuning fork for our still family choir
Like Joseph Wright of Derby's astrological lecture
Casts rings of benediction round the aged.
I never tire of ocean's quarrelling,
Its silence, its raw voice,
Nor of these half-lit, windy leaves, gesticulating higher
'Rejoice, rejoice ...'

But there's an old fish, a monster
Of primal fiction that drives barrelling
Undersea, too old to make a splash,
To which I'm hooked!
Through daydream, through nightmare trolling
Me so deep that no lights flash
There but the plankton's drifting, phosphorescent stars.

I see with its aged eyes,
Its dead green, glaucous gaze,
And I'm elsewhere, far as
I shall ever be from you whom I behold now
Dear family, dear friends, by this still glow,
The lantern's ring that the sea's
Never extinguished.
Your voices curl in the shell of my ear.

All day you've watched
The sea-rock like a loom
Shuttling its white wool, sheer Penelope!
The coals lit, the sky glows, an oven.
Heart into heart carefully laid
Like bread.
This is the fire that draws us by our dread
Of loss, the furnace door of heaven.

At night we have heard
The forest, an ocean of leaves, drowning her children,
Still, we belong here. There's Venus. We are not yet lost.

Like you, I preferred
The firefly's starlike little
Lamp, mining, a question,
To the highway's brightly multiplying beetles.

Coral

This coral's shape echoes the hand
It hollowed. Its

Immediate absence is heavy. As pumice,
As your breast in my cupped palm.

Sea-cold, its nipple rasps like sand,
Its pores, like yours, shone with salt sweat.

Bodies in absence displace their weight,
And your smooth body, like none other

Creates an exact absence like this stone
Set on a table with a whitening wrack

Of souvenirs. It dares my hand
To claim what lovers' hands have never known:

The nature of the body of another.

Codicil

Schizophrenic, wrenched by two styles,
one a hack's hired prose, I earn
my exile. I trudge this sickle, moonlit beach for miles, .

tan, burn
to slough off
this love of ocean that's self-love.

To change your language you must change your life.

I cannot right old wrongs.
Waves tire of horizon and return.
Gulls screech with rusty tongues

Above the beached, rotting pirogues,
they were a venomous beaked cloud at Charlotteville.

Once I thought love of country was enough,
now, even I chose, there's no room at the trough.

I watch the best minds root like dogs
for scraps of favour.
I am nearing middle-

age, burnt skin
peels from my hand like paper, onion-thin,
like Peer Gynt's riddle.

At heart there's nothing, not the dread
of death. I know too many dead.
They're all familiar, all in character,

even how they died. On fire,
the flesh no longer fears that furnace mouth
of earth,

that kiln or ashpit of the sun,
nor this clouding, unclouding sickle moon
whitening this beach again like a blank page.

All its indifference is a different rage.

The Gulf
and other poems

EBB

Year round, year round, we'll ride
this treadmill whose frayed tide
fretted with mud

leaves our suburban shoreline littered
with rainbow muck, the afterbirth
of industry, past scurf-

streaked bungalows
and pioneer factory;
but, blessedly, it narrows

through a dark aisle
of fountaining, gold coconuts, an oasis
marked for the yellow Caterpillar tractor.

We'll watch this shovelled too, but as we file
through its swift-wickered shade there always is
some island schooner netted in its weave

like a lamed heron
an oil-crippled gull;
a few more yards upshore

and it heaves free,
it races the horizon
with us, railed to one law,

ruled, like the washed-up moon
to circle her lost zone,
her radiance thinned.

The palm fronds signal wildly in the wind,
but we are bound elsewhere,
from the last sacred wood.

The schooner's out too far,
too far that boyhood.
Sometimes I turn to see

the schooner, crippled, try to tread the air,
the moon break in sere sail,
but without envy.

For safety, each sunfall,
the wildest of us all
mortgages life to fear.

And why not? From this car
there's terror enough in the habitual,
miracle enough in the familiar. Sure ...

THE CORN GODDESS

Silence asphalts the highway, our tires hiss
like serpents, of God's touching weariness,
his toil unfinished, while in endless rows
the cabbage fields, like lilies, spin in air;
his flags rot, and the monkey god's nerves rattle
lances in rage. Human rags tend cattle
more venal every year, and chrome-tooled cars
lathered like estate horses nose the shallows.
At dusk the Presbyterian cattle-bell
collects lean, charcoal-brittle elders,
stalled in their vision of a second hell,
as every crossroad crucifies its sect
of bell-voiced, bell-robed sisters, god-gelders
baying for self-respect. But, over braziers
of roasting corn while their shucked souls
evenly char, the sybil glows. Her seal's skin
shines like drizzled asphalt, in that grin
all knowledges burnt out. Jeer, but their souls
catch an elation fiercer than your desolate
envy; from their fanned, twisting coals
their shrieks crackle and fly. The sparks
are sorrowing upward though they die.

METAMOPHOSES

I · MOON

Resisting poetry I am becoming a poem.
O lolling Orphic head silently howling,
my own head rises from its surf of cloud.

Slowly my body grows a single sound,
slowly I become
a bell,
an oval, disembodied vowel,
I grow, an owl,
an aureole, white fire.

I watch the moonstruck image of the moon burn,
a candle mesmerized by its own aura,
and turn
my hot, congealing face, towards that forked mountain
which wedges the drowned singer.

That frozen glare,
that morsured, classic petrifaction.
Haven't you sworn off such poems for this year,
and no more on the moon?

Why are you gripped by demons of inaction?
Whose silence shrieks so soon?

II · SERPENT

Behind this porous skull, cold as this star,
below membranous veins the serpent drowses.
The quartz eyes glint from its adze-heavy head.

Leisurely as evil, rehearsing vice,
conducting its self-seducing sibilance,
the only creature without hands, it broods upon

the obese split and coupling of time
when its forked tongue rhymed all,
crotch, apple, breath, and you, forked fool, approaching

this coral oracle to hear how it once sung
of lust, of wisdom from God's sorrow wrung,
who step back, stung.

III · CAT

As carefully as
old Carlos Williams's cat's foot
forks the air,
and the curled tines, sheathing, back
from some pneumatic
nothing,

my nerves feeler each crack
in that blue sky.
It is going to pieces.
There is a stain
there, from the brain,
on that blue plaster.
Spell it, it spells
disaster. I'll

hoard, I'll huddle, I'll
contain myself.
Between this bed and mirror is
a mould I must inhabit.
It itches, it is ill.
To be a bridge, they said,
all you need do is keep still,

to surrender the ill-
usion that mirrors crouch, clothes
wait from their gibbet.
The green eyes socket
every action like a pinball.
She coils around some quiet
which is inward.

Finely she ovals
her fine, ringing teeth.
Their silent yowl.

The green eyes swallow yours,
they gulp, replete.
Waking, each hair is stirred.
I feel my body walking,
silent, furred.
Those feet.
Whose are those feet?

IV · HAWK

(for *Oliver Jackman*)

Leaves shudder the drizzle's shine
like a treng-ka-treng from the cuatros,
beads fly from the tension line.
Gabilan, ay, gabilan,
high shadow, pitiless!
The old men without teeth,
rum-guzzlers, country fiddlers,
their rum-heads golden lakes
of a fabulous Yucatan,
Gabilan, ay, gabilan!

Caribs, like toothless tigers;
talons raking, a flash,
arrows like twanging wires,
catgut and ocelot,
merciless, that is man,
Gabilan, eh, gabilan?
Arima to Sangre Grande,
your wings like extended hands,
a grandee waltzing alone,
alone, to the old parang.

Gabilan, ay, gabilan,
the negroes, bastards, mestizos,
proud of their Spanish blood,
of the flesh, dripping like wires,
praising your hook, gabilan.
Above their slack mouths the hawk
floats tautly out of the cedars,
leaves the limbs shaking.

Slaves yearn for their master's talons,
the spur and the cold, gold eyes,
for the whips, whistling like wires,

time for our turn, gabilan!
But this hawk above Rampanalgas
rasps the sea with raw cries.
Hawks have no music.

JUNTA

The sun's brass clamp electrifies a skull
kept shone since he won Individual
of the Year, their first year on the road,
as Vercingetorix And His Barbarous Horde;
lurching from lounge to air-conditioned lounge
with the crazed soldier ant's logistic skill
of pause as capture, he stirs again to plunge,
his brain's antennae on fire through the black ants
milling and mulling through each city fissure;
banlon-cool limers, shopgirls, Civil Servants.
'Caesar', the hecklers siegheil, 'Julius Seizure!'
He fakes an epileptic, clenched salute,
taking their tone, is no use getting vex,
some day those brains will squelch below his boot
as sheaves of swords hoist Vercingetorix!

So that day bursts to bugling cocks, the sun's gong
clangs the coup, a church, a bank explodes
and, bullet-headed with his cow-horned gang
of marabunta hordes, he hits the road.
Dust powders the white dead in Woodford Square;
his black, khaki canaille, panting for orders,
surge round the kiosk, then divide to hear
him clomp up silence louder than the roars
of rapine. Silence. Dust. A microphone
crackles the tinfoil quiet. On its paws
the beast mills, basilisk-eyed, for its one
voice. He clears his gorge and feels the bile
of rhetoric rising. Enraged that every clause
'por la patria, la muerte' resounds
the same, he fakes a frothing fit and shows his wounds,
while, as the cold sheaves heighten, his eyes fix
on one black, bush-haired convict's widening smile.

MASS MAN

Through a great lion's head clouded by mange
a black clerk growls.
Next, a gold-wired peacock withholds a man,
a fan, flaunting its oval, jewelled eyes,
What metaphors!
What coruscating, mincing fantasies!

Hector Mannix, water-works clerk San Juan, has entered a lion,
Boysie, two golden mangoes bobbing for breastplates, barges
like Cleopatra down her river, making style.
'Join us' they shout, 'O God, child, you can't dance?'
but somewhere in that whirlwind's radiance
a child, rigged like a bat, collapses, sobbing.

But I am dancing, look, from an old gibbet
my bull-whipped body swings, a metronome!
Like a fruit-bat dropped in the silk cotton's shade
my mania, my mania is a terrible calm.

Upon your penitential morning,
some skull must rub its memory with ashes,
some mind must squat down howling in your dust,
some hand must crawl and recollect your rubbish,
someone must write your poems.

MIRAMAR

There'll be no miracle tonight; by the third drink
you can tell. The nerves deaden from steel
or a hollow sax. I look through the window:
a bus goes by like an empty hospital,
and turn. The stripper's spinning, pink
tits, falsies in a false light, her crotch's
mechanical lurch is her own rut, and think
of the night I almost burned my balls
off with some abrasive, powdery chemical
and in the next ward of the teaching hospital
would listen all night to the clenched, stuck
howl of a child dying of lockjaw. Clench, hold
on to what you have. After a while, this whole,
slow grinding circus doesn't give a fuck.
There is nowhere to go. You'd better go.

EXILE

Wind-haired, mufflered
against dawn, you watched the herd
of migrants ring the deck
from steerage. Only the funnel
bellowing, the gulls who peck
waste from the ploughed channel
knew that you had not come
to England; you were home.

Even her wretched weather
was poetry. Your scarred leather
suitcase held that first
indenture, to her Word,
but, among cattle docking, that rehearsed
calm meant to mark you from the herd
shook, calf-like, in her cold.

Never to go home again,
for this was home! The windows
leafed through history to the beat
of a school ballad, but the train
soon changed its poetry to the prose
of narrowing, pinched eyes you could not enter,
to the gas-ring, the ringing Students' Centre,
to the soiled, icy sheet.

One night, near rheum-eyed windows
your memory kept pace with winter's
pages, piled in drifts,
till Spring, which slowly lifts
the heart, broke into prose
and suns you had forgotten
blazoned from barrows.

And earth began to look
as you remembered her,
herons, like sea-gulls flock-
ed to the salted furrow,
the bellowing, smoky bullock
churned its cane sea,
a world began to pass
through your pen's eye,
between bent grasses and one word
for the bent rice.

And now, some phrase
caught in the parenthesis
of highway quietly states
its title, and an ochre trace
of flags and carat huts opens
at Chapter One,
the bullock's strenuous ease is mirrored
in a clear page of prose,
a forest is compressed in a blue coal,
or burns in graphite fire,
invisibly your ink nourishes
leaf after leaf the furrowed villages
where the smoke flutes
and the brittle pages
of the Ramayana stoke the mulch fires;

the arrowing, metal
highways head nowhere,
the tabla and the sitar amplified,
the Path unrolling like a dirty bandage,
the cinema-hoardings leer
in language half the country cannot read.

Yet, when dry winds rattle
the flags whose bamboo lances bend
to Hanuman, when, like chattel
folded in a cloth-knot, the debased
brasses are tremblingly placed

on flaking temple lintels,
when the god stamps his bells
and smoke writhes its blue arms
for your lost India,

the old men, threshing rice,
rheum-eyed, pause,
their brown gaze flecked with chaff,
their loss chafed by the raw
whine of the cinema-van calling the countryside
to its own dark devotions,
summoning the drowned from oceans
of deep cane. The hymn
to Mother India whores its lie.
Your memory walks by its soft-spoken
path, as flickering, broken,
Saturday jerks past like a cheap film.

THE TRAIN

On one hand, harrowed England,
iron, an airfield's mire,
on the other, fire-
gutted trees, a hand
raking the carriage windows.

Where was my randy white grandsire from?
He left here a century ago
to found his 'farm',
and, like a thousand others,
drunkenly seed their archipelago.
Through dirty glass
his landscape fills through my face.

Black with despair
he set his flesh on fire,
blackening, a tree of flame.
That's hell enough for here.
His blood burns through me as this engine races,
my skin sears like a hairshirt with his name.

On the bleak Sunday platform
the guiltless, staring faces
divide like tracks before me as I come.
Like you, grandfather, I cannot change places,
I am half-home.

HOMAGE TO EDWARD THOMAS

Formal, informal, by a country's cast
topography delineates its verse,
erects the classic bulk, for rigid contrast
of sonnet, rectory or this manor-house
dourly timbered against these sinuous
Downs, defines the formal and informal prose
of Edward Thomas's poems which make this garden
return its subtle scent of Edward Thomas
in everything here hedged or loosely grown.
Lines which you once dismissed as tenuous
because they would not howl or overwhelm,
as crookedly grave-bent, or cuckoo-dreaming,
seemingly dissoluble as this Sussex down
harden in their indifference, like this elm.

A CHANGE OF SKIN

(for *Laurence Goldstraw*)

The fog, a sheepdog circling, bared
its teeth from slavering hedges
at the dark, sheepskin-collared

stranger; then coldly it grew clear
as those green, lucent panes
of England that his fear

of history was its lack. Pins
of fine rain prickled his skin's
horror of that cold, and the bone

shuddered from deep-tutored
awe of arrogant stone,
as when dark tribes ground to his tread,

mulch-black and brown leaves seethed
nourishing England. In an air
cold as iron, he freely breathed

the exhilaration of pure hatred;
how on grey mornings, when like hair
prickling the scalp, the trees stir

memory of their irresolute temperature
now kind, now cold, he waits,
knowing its fire purifies with sweat,

for the unsubtle, unequivocal sun,
for heat that shapes his shadow surely like the blow from glare to sudden

shade, from fear to fondness of a fever
shed, like history cured of hatred,
like life of literature.

THE GULF

(for Jack and Barbara Harrison)

The airport coffee tastes less of America.
Sour, unshaven, dreading the exertion
of tightening, racked nerves fuelled with liquor,

some smoky, resinous Bourbon,
the body, buckling at its casket hole,
a roar like last night's blast racing its engines,

watches the fumes of the exhausted soul
as the trans-Texas jet, screeching, begins
its flight and friends diminish. So, to be aware

of the divine union the soul detaches
itself from created things. 'We're in the air,'
the Texan near me grins. All things: these matches

from LBJ's campaign hotel, this rose
given me at dawn in Austin by a child,
this book of fables by Borges, its prose

a stalking, moonlit tiger. What was willed
on innocent, sun-streaked Dallas, the beast's claw
curled round that hairspring rifle is revealed

on every page as lunacy or feral law;
circling that wound we leave Love Field.
Fondled, these objects conjure hotels,

quarrels, new friendships, brown limbs
nakedly moulded as these autumn hills
memory penetrates as the jet climbs

the new clouds over Texas; their home means
an island suburb, forest, mountain water;
they are the simple properties for scenes

whose joy exhausts like grief, scenes where we learn,
exchanging the least gifts, this rose, this napkin,
that those we love are objects we return,

that this lens on the desert's wrinkled skin
has priced our flesh, all that we love in pawn
to that brass ball, that the gifts, multiplying

clutter and choke the heart, and that I shall
watch love reclaim its things as I lie dying.
My very flesh and blood! Each seems a petal

shrivelling from its core. I watch them burn,
by the nerves' flare I catch their skeletal
candour! Best never to be born

the great dead cry. Their works shine on our shelves,
by twilight we tour their gilded, gravestone spines,
and read until the lamplit page revolves

to a white stasis whose detachment shines
like a propeller's rainbowed radiance.
Circling like us; no comfort for their loves!

I I

The cold glass darkens. Elizabeth wrote once
that we make glass the image of our pain;
I watch clouds boil past the cold, sweating pane

above the Gulf. All styles yearn to be plain
as life. The face of the loved object under glass
is plainer still. Yet, somehow, at this height,

above this cauldron boiling with its wars,
our old earth, breaking to familiar light,
that cloud-bound mummy with self-healing scars

peeled of her cerements again looks new;
some cratered valley heals itself with sage,
through that grey, fading massacre a blue

light-hearted creek flutes of some siege
to the amnesia of drumming water.
Their cause is crystalline: the divine union

of these detached, divided States, whose slaughter
darkens each summer now, as one by one,
the smoke of bursting ghettos clouds the glass

down every coast where filling-station signs
proclaim the Gulf, an air, heavy with gas,
sickens the state, from Newark to New Orleans.

III

Yet the South felt like home. Wrought balconies,
the sluggish river with its tidal drawl,
the tropic air charged with the extremities

of patience, a heat heavy with oil,
canebrakes, that legendary jazz. But fear
thickened my voice, that strange, familiar soil

prickled and barbed the texture of my hair,
my status as a secondary soul.
The Gulf, your gulf, is daily widening,

each blood-red rose warns of that coming night
when there's no rock cleft to go hidin' in
and all the rocks catch fire, when that black might,

their stalking, moonless panthers turn from Him
whose voice they can no more believe, when the black X's
mark their passover with slain seraphim.

IV

The Gulf shines, dull as lead. The coast of Texas
glints like a metal rim. I have no home
as long as summer bubbling to its head

boils for that day when in the Lord God's name
the coals of fire are heaped upon the head
of all whose gospel is the whip and flame,

age after age, the uninstructing dead.

ELEGY

Our hammock swung between Americas
we miss you, Liberty. Che's
bullet-riddled body falls,
and those who cried the Republic must first die
to be reborn are dead,
the freeborn citizen's ballot in the head.
Still, everybody wants to go to bed
with Miss America. And, if there's no bread,
let them eat cherry pie.

But the old choice of running, howling, wounded
wolf-deep in her woods,
while the white papers snow on
genocide is gone;
no face can hide
its public, private pain,
wincing, already statued.

Some splintered arrowhead lodged in her brain
sets the black singer howling in his bear trap
shines young eyes with the brightness of the mad,
tires the old with her residual sadness;
and yearly lilacs in her dooryards bloom,
and the cherry orchard's surf
blinds Washington and whispers
to the assassin in his furnished room
of an ideal America, whose flickering screens
show, in slow herds, the ghosts of the Cheyennes
scuffling across the staked and wired plains
with whispering, rag-bound feet,

while the farm couple framed in their Gothic door
like Calvin's saints, waspish, pragmatic, poor,
gripping the devil's pitchfork
stare rigidly towards the immortal wheat.

June 6th, 1968

POSTCARDS

I · WASHINGTON

... the chilling blast
of a vault opening,
the iron light deflected from a shield,
the ringing reticence of marble boulevards,
the cool of autumn's air-conditioning.

The earnest, tilted face of President Johnson
wincing with concern,
and only blocks away, addresses me
directly from the console TV,
lined, habituated to crisis :
problems of space,
our child's wish for the moon,

while bombs of sumac burst below my window
and the live oaks catch fire,
and saffron beeches, gay
as a Buddhist's robes,
charred,
drop their rags, naked.

II · MAYARO

here, the season's dead;
the bleached beach-huts, the summer bungalows boarded,
their eyes sealed from devilish sand,
their deck chairs mired in dunes.
Almond leaves rake the dead terrace.

THE ATLANTIS BEACH HOTEL
hoards two lost souls,
its population vanished without trace

except where its fabled shore
is littered with the puffed, violet
prophylactics of Portuguese-man-o-war.

BLUES

Those five or six young guys
hunched on the stoop
that oven-hot summer night
whistled me over. Nice
and friendly. So, I stop.
MacDougal or Christopher
Street in chains of light.

A summer festival. Or some
saint's. I wasn't too far from
home, but not too bright
for a nigger, and not too dark,
I figured we were all
one, wop, nigger, jew,
besides, this wasn't Central Park.
I'm coming on too strong? You figure
right! They beat this yellow nigger
black and blue.

Yeah. During all this, scared
in case one used a knife,
I hung my olive-green, just-bought
sports coat on a fire-plug.
I did nothing. They fought
each other, really. Life
gives them a few kicks,
that's all. The spades, the spicks.

My face smashed in, my bloody mug
pouring, my olive-branch jacket saved
from cuts and tears,
I crawled four flights upstairs.
Sprawled in the gutter, I
remember a few watchers waved
loudly, and one kid's mother shouting

like 'Jackie' or 'Terry',
'Now that's enough!'
It's nothing really.
They don't get enough love.

You know they wouldn't kill
you. Just playing rough,
like young America will.
Still, it taught me something
about love. If it's so tough,
forget it.

AIR

There has been romance, but it has been the romance of pirates and out-laws. The natural graces of life do not show themselves under such con-ditions. There are no people there in the true sense of the word, with a character and purpose of their own.

Froude: *The Bow of Ulysses*

The unheard, omnivorous
jaws of this rain forest
not merely devour all,
but allow nothing vain;
they never rest,
grinding their disavowal
of human pain.

Long, long before us,
those hot jaws like an oven
steaming, were open
to genocide; they devoured
two minor yellow races and
half of a black;
in the word made flesh of God
all entered that gross, un-
discriminating stomach;

the forest is unconverted,
because that shell-like noise
which roars like silence, or
ocean's surpliced choirs
entering its nave, to a censer
of swung mist, is not
the rustling of prayer
but nothing; milling air,
a faith, infested, cannibal,
which eats gods, which devoured

the god-refusing Carib, petal
by golden petal, then forgot,
and the Arawak
who leaves not the lightest fern-trace
of his fossil to be cultured
by black rock,

but only the rusting cries
of a rainbird, like a hoarse
warrior summoning his race
from vaporous air
between this mountain ridge
and the vague sea
where the lost exodus
of corials sunk without trace –

There is too much nothing here.

GUYANA

I

The surveyor straightens from his theodolite.
'Spirit-level,' he scrawls, and instantly
the ciphers staggering down their columns
are soldier ants, their panic radiating in the shadow
of a new god arriving over Aztec anthills.

The sun has sucked his brain pith-dry.
His vision whirls with dervishes, he is dust.
Like an archaic photographer, hooded in shade,
he crouches, screwing a continent to his eye.

The vault that balances on a grass blade,
the nerve-cracked ground too close for the word 'measureless',
for the lost concept, 'man',
revolve too slowly for the fob-watch of his world,
for the tidal markings of the five-year plan.

Ant-sized to God, god to an ant's eyes,
shouldering science he begins to tread
himself, a world that must be measured in three days.

The frothing shallows of the river,
the forest so distant that it tires of blue,
the merciless idiocy of green, green ...

a shape dilates towards him through the haze.

Together they walked through a thickness pinned with birds
silent as rags, grackles and flycatchers mostly,
shaking words from their heads.

their beaks aimed at one target, the clotting sun.
Tight, with the tension of arrows.

Dark climbed their knees until their heads were dark,
The wind, wave-muscled, kept its steady mowing.
Thoughts fell from him like leaves.

He followed, that was all,
his mind, one step behind,
pacing the poem, going where it was going.

'Man, all the men in that damned country mad!'
There was the joke on W. and Mayakovsky.
There was the charred bush of a man found in the morning,
there was the burgher's glare of whitewashed houses
out-staring guilt,
                    there was the anthropologist
dropping on soft pads from the thorn branches
to the first stance hearing the vowels
fur in his throat the hoarse
pebbles of consonants rattling his parched gullet,
there was the poet howling in vines of syntax
and the surveyor
dumbstruck by a stone;
                        at noon, the ferment
of white air, lilies and canal water
heavy as bush rum, then amber
saddening twilights without ice.
A fist should smash the glare of skylight open.
In the asylum the prisoners slept like snakes,
their eyes wide open.
                    They wait.
All of us wait.

IV · THE FALLS

Their barrelling roar would open like a white oven
for him,
who was a spirit now, who could not burn or drown.

Surely in that 'smoke that thundered' there was a door –
but the noise boiled to the traffic of a white town
of bicycles, pigeons, bells, smoke, trains at the rush hour

revolving to this roar.
He was a flower,
weightless. He would float down.

V · A MAP OF THE CONTINENT

The lexicographer in his cell records the life and death of books;
the naked buck waits at the edge of the world.

One hefts a pen, the other a bone spear;
between them curls a map,
between them curl the vigorous, rotting leaves,

shelves forested with titles, trunks that wait for names –
it pierces knowledge, the spear-flash!
the fish thrashing green air
on a pen's hook,

above the falls reciting its single flower.

The lexicographer's lizard eyes are curled
in sleep. The Amazonian Indian enters them.

Between the Rupunini and Borges,
between the fallen pen-tip and the spear-head
thunders, thickens and shimmers the one age of the world.

(i)

Begun, with its own impulse of destruction,
this elegy that chokes its canals
like the idle, rotting lilies of this frontier,
its lines that rust, however shiningly they thrust forward, like the
    elementary railway
besieging the whitewashed city
that reminds the poet on his balcony of thunder.

Begun, with a brown heron,
like the one I named for an actor,
its emblem answering a question with a question:
'What bird is that,
whose is that woman,
what will become of their country?'

If the neck of the heron is condemned to its question,
if the woman is silent,
and if, at the most appropriate hour
of a rose-scrim twilight budding with onion domes
like the gaze of clerkish guerrillas hazed by an epoch,
if nothing comes,
if no one ever escapes,
if the shoreline longs sadly for spires,
there is nothing left for us
but to make these coarse lilies lotuses,
for filth to contemplate its own reflection.

Cycle bells startle the pigeons.
The air has been cleared of hawks,
and the bourgeois gurgling like canals
reminisce over carrion.

Spires walk the sea-wall.

The wind unwraps them to wires.
They recede, skeletal, skeletal,
the streets have grown ordinary as heroes.

And the prose of polemics grows, spreading lianas' of syntax
for the rootless surveyor,
the thunderous falls have been measured,
the thickening girth of the continent has been buttoned
till a man knows his weight to the stone,
his worth to the inch,
yet imagines he hears in his hair
the rain horses crossing savannahs
and his pores prickle like water.

The towns are clogged at their edges,
a glutinous dialect chokes the slum's canals,
and the white, finical houses
lift their lace skirts, stepping over the creeks.

Hawsers have lifted the country on delicate ankles.
The dead face of an orator revolves by lamplight,
the glazed scar itches for blood.

The girl waits in the wings, heron-still;
she will rise to the roar of the playhouse
its applauding cataract,

and the train rusts, travelling to a few sad sparks,
and the muck, and the tins, and the sogged placards choke
the sad, motionless green of the canals.

(ii)

So, safest, I had unimagined time;
thus we forget our element
like a fish that gasps with surprise on the nib of a hook.

There was always death,
but that came in the cheapest pricklings,
in old songs, in the amazed fading of letters,
in the change in one's penmanship:
how an l wavers like a single lily shaken
by a stone, how an r reaches, rightly, to touch
some vertical end,

and at startling moments, the rattle of a kite
on a pluperfect sky.
Now words like 'azure' for instance, suddenly touch,
such homilies as 'infinite' momentarily burn,
and for these lined eyes to widen
the heart, when to have written 'heart'
was to know a particular spasm –
how an old rock could spout such crystalline gibberish
amuses me, like the exact dancing of machines.

Nothing could turn my head, not the night moth,
like a nun beating her prison, but now pain comes
where I least expect it:
in the hissing of bicycle tires on drizzled asphalt,
in the ambush of little infinities
as supple with longing as the word 'horizon'.
Sad is the felon's love for the scratched wall,
beautiful the exhaustion of old towels,
and the patience of dented saucepans
seems mortally comic.

All these predictions do not disappoint but bring us nearer.
They uphold history like a glass of water.
If the poem begins to shrivel
I no longer distend my heart,
for I know how profound is the folding of a napkin
by a woman whose hair will go white,
age, that says more than an ocean,
I know how final is the straightening of a sheet
between lovers who have never lain, the heart-breaking curve
of a woman, her back bent, concerned
with the finical precisions of farewell.

(iii)

And there I entered your green, sibilant Russias,
those canes that like wheat must blacken after harvest,
and I honoured your dead, those few
arranged in postures for your great elegies,
who are what they were, not heroes, merely men.

The age will know its own name when it comes,
as love will find its breath softly expelling
'was I like this?'
with the same care, the precise exhilaration
with which the heron's foot pronounces 'earth'.

What if, impulsive, delicate bird,
one instinct made you rise
out of this life, into another's,
then from another's, circling to your own?
You are folded in my eyes,
whose irises will open
to a white sky with bird and woman gone.

CHE

In this dark-grained news-photograph, whose glare
is rigidly composed as Caravaggio's,
the corpse glows candle-white on its cold altar –

its stone Bolivian Indian butcher's slab –
stare till its waxen flesh begins to harden
to marble, to veined, Andean iron;
from your own fear, *cabron*, its pallor grows;

it stumbled from your doubt, and for your pardon
burnt in brown trash, far from the embalming snows.

NEGATIVES

A newsclip; the invasion of Biafra:
black corpses wrapped in sunlight
sprawled on the white glare entering what's its name –
the central city?

        Someone who's white
illuminates the news behind the news,
his eyes flash with, perhaps, pity:
'The Ibos, you see, are like the Jews,
very much the situation in Hitler's Germany,
I mean the Hausas' resentment.' I try to see.

I never knew you Christopher Okigbo,
I saw you when an actor screamed 'The tribes!
the tribes!' I catch
the guttering, flare-lit
faces of Ibos,
stuttering, bug-eyed
prisoners of some drumhead tribunal.

The soldiers' helmeted shadows
could have been white, and yours
one of those sun-wrapped bodies on the white road
entering ... the tribes, the tribes, their shame –
that central city, Christ, what is its name?

LANDFALL, GRENADA

(for Robert Head, mariner)

Where you are rigidly anchored,
the groundswell of blue foothills, the blown canes
surging to cumuli cannot be heard;
like the slow, seamless ocean,
one motion folds the grass where you were lowered,
and the tiered sea
whose grandeurs you detested
climbs out of sound.

Its moods held no mythology
for you, it was a working-place
of tonnage and ruled stars;
you chose your landfall with a mariner's
casual certainty,
calm as that race
into whose heart you harboured;
your death was a log's entry,
your suffering held the strenuous
reticence of those
whose rites are never public,
hating to impose, to offend.
Deep friend, teach me to learn
such ease, such landfall going,
such mocking tolerance of those
neat, gravestone elegies
that rhyme our end.

HOMECOMING: ANSE LA RAYE

(for Garth St Omer)

Whatever else we learned
at school, like solemn Afro-Greeks eager for grades,
of Helen and the shades
of borrowed ancestors,
there are no rites
for those who have returned,
only, when her looms fade,
drilled in our skulls, the doom-
surge-haunted nights,
only this well-known passage
under the coconuts' salt-rusted
swords, these rotted
leathery sea-grape leaves,
the seacrabs' brittle helmets, and
this barbecue of branches, like the ribs
of sacrificial oxen on scorched sand;
only this fish-gut reeking beach
whose spindly, sugar-headed children race
whose starved, pot-bellied children race
pelting up from the shallows
because your clothes,
your posture
seem a tourist's.
They swarm like flies
round your heart's sore.

Suffer them to come,
entering your needle's eye,
knowing whether they live or die,
what others make of life will pass them by
like that far silvery freighter
threading the horizon like a toy;
for once, like them,
you wanted no career
but this sheer light, this clear,

infinite, boring, paradisal sea,
but hoped it would mean something to declare
today, I am your poet, yours,
all this you knew,
but never guessed you'd come.
to know there are homecomings without home.

You give them nothing.
Their curses melt in air.
The black cliffs scowl,
the ocean sucks its teeth,
like that dugout canoe
a drifting petal fallen in a cup,
with nothing but its image,
you sway, reflecting nothing.
The freighter's silvery ghost
is gone, the children gone.
Dazed by the sun
you trudge back to the village
past the white, salty esplanade
under whose palms, dead
fishermen move their draughts in shade,
crossing, eating their islands,
and one, with a politician's
ignorant, sweet smile, nods,
as if all fate
swayed in his lifted hand.

D'AUBAIGNAN

(for Grace Augustin)

Here, cries the child, the river's mirror drowned me!
Smiling at first, it went
too fast, viciously cold.
It is so with rivers and friends.
I was a hand stroking a burnished serpent.
Ten or eleven; heaven
was nearer; the yellowing, old estate house crumbled like cake,
stencilled with fern-prints, veiled in mosquito nets;
after the virgin lamp's light paled
there were moths dead by morning and moths
staggering through the breaking gauze
of vapour, water-logged as the souls
of schoolboys climbing from old water-holes.
His thin ghost, doubtless, coils
from the mist where he would gaze
the last time on his lack of sin,
the worst: to outlast his father
to live till he could write
lines finer than his own.
Burdened with both world's weight
he should have sunk like a stone.

Now, such ambition thins
like mist, but not my terror,
my knowledge of rivers and friends;
no heaven is ruled as neat
as those blue copybooks in which he wrote
those lines which never held
him, as he yelled,
'Father, father, I'll drown!'
I am used to those cries,
I have watched him go down
coldly, a smiling coward,
envying him what is called the 'easiest death',
in coiling glass that steams when I have showered,
I watch his father with a drowned child's eyes.

THE RIVER

was one, once;
reduced by circumstance
the Council tends it. Once

it could roar through town,
foul-mouthed, brown-muscled, brazenly
drunk, a raucous country-bookie,

but lately it has grown
too footloose for this settlement
of shacks, rechristened a city;

its strength wasted on gutters,
it never understood the age,
what progress meant,

so its clear, brown integument
shrivelled, its tongue stutters
through the official language,

it surrenders its gutturals
to the stern, stone Victorian bridge;
reclaimed, it dies a little

daily, it crawls towards a sea
curdled with oil-slick, its force
thins like the peasantry,

it idles like those resinous
wrinkled woodsmen, the country
reek still on them, hoarse

with municipal argument,
who, falling suddenly silent
on wire-bright afternoons, reflect

on mornings when a torrent
roared down their gorges, and
no one gave a damn what the words meant.

TO THE HOTEL SAINT ANTOINE

At dawn, dead-tired from dancing in the streets,
we fell on its white, wooden rooms to rest
till the next day's parades;

indigo darkness thinned, the north-east trades
wind I'd forgotten, like a beast,
foraged its thicket.

I tracked its trough downhill by the leaves churn,
the power it embodied visible
as I, who had returned, a voluble ghost,

as that dead friend, or the first love I lost,
but whether in grief or rage its branches tossed,
joy next day shook the wretched, flag-girt town.

Now, back in our own house, stirred by that noise,
which while you slept, pawed at our hotel windows,
I watch how, from your trunk, our daughter grows

within that casual mimicry of death,
of Margaret branching to Elizabeth,
and envy the wind's power to rejoice

that all are wrapped within earth's winding sheet,
sailing with her, in these cloud-coloured shrouds;
that the air is at war, that every prism

of nothing renews its Thermopylae,
the caged inch netted with furies. Nothing consumes.
A fistful of home earth fumes

with the rose of a girl, the grass is
the hair of some skull, a razor
opens the grave's wrist.

Dead and dreaming exchange pities.
Huddled, till dawn in wooden, echoing rooms,
they share their different and indifferent cities.

GOODNIGHT LADIES, GOODNIGHT
SWEET LADIES ...

Even there the chasm yawns, between twin bed
and boredom; like lilies her mind drifts
backwards, oh, towards some lost romance; his
careers rakehell through red, flickering stews
through every brothel of imagination
where lewd, insatiable harlots are spread
white, or a black, tangled harem dances.
This is the last of nature's wedding gifts.
Celibates may rise in righteous indignation;
only to newly-weds will this be news.

THE CELL

Woman, wasp-waisted, then wasp-tongued,
hissing to enemies how much I wronged
you, how just you were! We would secrete
in every cell, each separate room
the stink and stigma of my name,
and nothing, not the bedside flame
charring in coils by the child's net
could calm your virulent regret
or my last effort, lust. You cried
against the poison charged inside
his flesh and yours, I prayed we'd clasp
each other fierce as coupling wasps,
as bitter-sweet it seemed to flesh
to die in self-stung martyrdom,
for mind and body bitten black
with shame to take its poison back,
to build, even in hate, a home,
in that hexagonal lace mesh
shuddering, exchanging venom.

SATURDAY MORNING AT THE FLYING CLUB

Jets like smoke-bleeding dragons scarved the air
on the sun's flashing lance-point, but for us,
crossing that breezy headland,
the small planes purred like pigeons in a square,
one strutted waddling almost to my hand;
at every roar
the sky shut trundling its iron door,
but we were free,
locked in each other's hands,
freer than lovers with their wives and husbands.

Now memory circles there,
a pigeon homing on a detail, a hawk
wheeling to fasten on some phrase
gripping that field of flowers whose name you knew,
that whole harbour and headland
hazing from distance like your eyes,
grey, or grey-blue,
already, then, it knew
the lancings of this poem,
its lines, its outlines, they were there
in the tiered waves,
the scarves and scallops of their virginal elation,
their joy shot higher,
and that charged silhouette of golden hair
against its yellow field, St Elmo's fire!

Joy balanced on its needle point of noon!
one needle stroke past twelve, it whirled
like the jet's roar
on its inflexible point of aerial law,
the pigeon homing, the hawk remarrying
the ringed wrist. O heart and sky
inflexible in their fidelity!
Ah patience, tiring
of a pain's pin glint into memory.

STAR

If, in the light of things, you fade
real, yet wanly withdrawn
to our determined and appropriate
distance, like the moon left on
all night among the leaves, may
you invisibly delight this house,
O star, doubly compassionate, who came
too soon for twilight, too late
for dawn, may your faint flame
strive with the worst in us
through chaos
with the passion of
plain day.

COLD SPRING HARBOUR

From feather-stuffed bolsters of cloud
falling on casual linen
the small shrieks soundlessly float.
The woods are lint-wreathed. Dawn
crackles like foil to the rake
of a field mouse nibbling, nibbling
its icing. The world is unwrapped
in cotton and you would tread wool
if you opened, quietly, whitely,
this door, like an old Christmas card
turned by a child's dark hand; did
he know it was dark then,
the magical brittle branches, the white house
collared in fur, the white world of men,
its bleeding gules and its berry drops?

Two prancing, immobile white ponies
no bigger than mice pulled a carriage
across soundless hillocks of cotton;
bells hasped to their necks didn't tinkle
though you begged God to touch them to life,
some white-haired old God who'd forgotten
or no longer trusted his miracles.
What urges you now towards this white,
snow-whipped woods is not memory
of that dark child's toys, not the card
of a season, forever foreign that went
over its ridges like a silent
sleigh. That was a child's sorrow, this is
child's play through which you cannot go,
dumbstruck at an open door,
stunned, fearing the strange violation
(because you are missing your children)
of perfect snow.

IN THE KITCHEN

She feels her eyelids narrowing
on one fierce, drifting speck
that splinters to a sorrowing
hymn of midges, or to mercurial
angels dancing on a pinhead,
she finds, week after week,
more friends among the dead;
they were not all angels; all
this is is the glittering note
of a tin penny flute
of a houseboy in the kitchen,
with 'when the saints, the saints'
stuck in its throat.

And the phrase note by note,
and one by one the dead,
and the grass, blade by blade,
begins to be remembered;
each hair upon that head
mother, is numbered, numbered;
numbered the tan, charcoal kitten's
wisps of fur; the mirror hazes
as your own vision brightens,
as the saints, one by one,
take their accustomed places.

O their faint, golden congregations
mother! O their ballooning, zephyr-
bugling cheeks, their shining patience!
When I could really kneel,
not stew in the imagination's
drab adulteries. I wait
each week like you, my own breath
bated, my faith stuck in my throat,

for father to come down. Husband,
take up your young wife's hand,
embrace this woman who has waited
since her first death for this.

LOVE IN THE VALLEY

The sun goes slowly blind.
It is this mountain, shrouding
the valley of the shadow,

widening like amnesia
evening dims the mind.
I shake my head in darkness,

it is a tree branched with cries,
a trash-can full of print.
Now, through the reddening squint

of leaves leaden as eyes,
a skein of drifting hair
like a twig, fallen on snow,

branches the blank pages.
I bring it close, and stare
in slow vertiginous darkness,

and now I drift elsewhere,
through hostile images,
of white and black, and look,

like a thaw-sniffing stallion, the head
of Pasternak emerges with its forelock,
his sinewy wrist a fetlock

pawing the frozen spring,
till his own hand has frozen
on the white page, heavy.

I ride through a white childhood
whose pines glittered with bracelets,
when I heard wolves, feared the black wood,

every wrist-aching brook
and the ice maiden
in Hawthorne's fairy book.

The hair melts into dark,
a question mark that led
where the untethered mind

strayed from its first track,
Now Hardy's sombre head
over which hailstorms broke

looms, like a weeping rock,
like wind, the tresses drift
and its familiar trace

tingles across the face
with its light lashes.
I feared the depth of whiteness,

I feared the numbing kiss
of those women of winter,
Bathsheba, Lara, Tess

whose tragedy made less
of life, whose love was more
than love or literature.

GIB HALL REVISITED

(for Wayne Brown)

In those raft-planked bunkhouses christened Gibraltar
by World War II D.P.s, as if they knew
we'd drift like displaced persons too, but even further
from Europe than the homesick, homeless Jew,
to that new world already tagged and named
what could we add but rhetoric, who had
less faith than the prophetically maimed?
A generation late, I sadden
that the brightest ones were sold
to a system, like those stars to Arabic,
that our first Christmas riots hid the sick
envy of Caliban for our master's gown
of ersatz ermine; fearing the fission
of red gown to black, of fire to ash, we moved
across dry campus grass in separate flames,
cold, unlit candles looking for one vision,
our red gowns wilted like poinsettia.
Now, in the black, processioned and approved,
old hands acknowledge us by our first names,
the red gowns mark the same betrayals down.

NEARING FORTY

(for John Figueroa)

The irregular combination of fanciful invention may delight awhile by that
novelty of which the common satiety of life sends us all in quest. But the
pleasures of sudden wonder are soon exhausted and the mind can only
repose on the stability of truth ...

Samuel Johnson

Insomniac since four, hearing this narrow,
rigidly-metred, early-rising rain
recounting, as if its coolness numbs the marrow,
that I am nearing forty, nearer the weak
vision thickening to a frosted pane,
nearer the day when I may judge my work
by the bleak modesty of middle-age
as a false dawn, fireless and average,
which would be just, because your life bled for
the household truth, the style past metaphor
that finds its parallels, however wretched
in simple, shining lines, in pages stretched
plain as a bleaching bedsheet under a guttering rainspout; glad for the sputter
of occasional insight, you who foresaw
ambition as a searing meteor
will fumble a damp match, and smiling, settle
for the dry wheezing of a dented kettle,
for vision narrower than a louvre's gap,
then watching your leaves thin, recall how deep
prodigious cynicism plants its seed,
gauges our seasons by this year's end rain
which, as greenhorns at school, we'd
call conventional for convectional
or you will rise and set your lines to work
with sadder joy but steadier elation,
until the night when you can really sleep,
measuring how imagination

ebbs, conventional as any water-clerk
who weighs the force of lightly-falling rain,
which, as the new moon moves it, does its work,
even when it seems to weep.

THE WALK

After hard rain the eaves repeat their beads,
those trees exhale your doubt like mantled tapers,
drop after drop, like a child's abacus
beads of cold sweat file from high tension wires,

pray for us, pray for this house, borrow your neighbour's
faith, pray for this brain that tires,
and loses faith in the great books it reads;
after a day spent prone, haemorrhaging poems,

each phrase peeled from the flesh in bandages,
arise, stroll on under a sky
sodden as kitchen laundry,

while the cats yawn behind their window frames,
lions in cages of their choice,
no further though, than your last neighbour's gates
figured with pearl. How terrible is your own

fidelity, O heart, O rose of iron!
When was your work more like a housemaid's novel,
some drenched soap-opera which gets
closer than yours to life? Only the pain,

the pain is real. Here's your life's end,
a clump of bamboos whose clenched
fist loosens its flowers, a track
that hisses through the rain-drenched

grove: abandon all, the work,
the pain of a short life. Startled, you move;
your house, a lion rising, paws you back.

HIC JACET

I

They'll keep on asking, why did you remain?
Not for the applauding rain
of hoarse and hungry thousands at whose centre
the politician opens like a poisonous flower,
not for the homecoming lecturer
gripping his lectern like a witness, ready to explain
the root's fixation with earth,
nor for that new race of dung beetles, frock-coated, iridescent
crawling over the people.
Before the people became popular
he loved them.

Nor to spite some winter-bitten novelist
praised for his accuracy of phlegm,
but for something rooted, unwritten
that gave us its benediction,
its particular pain,
that may move its clouds from that mountain,
that is packing its bags on that fiction
of our greatness, which, like the homecoming rain,
veers to a newer sea.

II

I loved them all, the names
of shingled, rusting towns, whose dawn
touches like metal,
I should have written poems on the Thames,
shivered through cities furred and cracked with ice,
spat, for their taste, in some barge-burdened river.

III

Convinced of the power of provincialism,
I yielded quietly my knowledge of the world

to a grey tub steaming with clouds of seraphim,
the angels and flags of the world,
and answer those who hiss, like steam, of exile,
this coarse soap-smelling truth:

I sought more power than you, more fame than yours,
I was more hermetic, I knew the commonweal,
I pretended subtly to lose myself in crowds
knowing my passage would alter their reflection,
I was that muscle shouldering the grass
through ordinary earth,
commoner than water I sank to lose my name,
this was my second birth.

Sea Grapes

Sea Grapes

That little sail in light
which tires of islands,
a schooner beating up the Caribbean

for home, could be Odysseus,
home-bound on the Aegean,
that father and husband's

longing, under gnarled sour grapes, is
like the adulterer hearing Nausicaa's name
in every gull's outcry;

This brings nobody peace. The ancient war
between obsession and responsibility
will never finish and has been the same

for the sea-wanderer or the one on shore
now wriggling on his sandals to walk home,
since Troy lost its old flame,

and the blind giant's boulder heaved the trough
from whose ground-swell the great hexameters come
to finish up as Caribbean surf.

The classics can console. But not enough.

The Virgins

Down the dead streets of sun-stoned Frederiksted,
the first freeport to die for tourism,
strolling at funeral pace, I am reminded
of life not lost to the American dream,
but my small-islander's simplicities,
can't better our new empire's civilized
exchange of cameras, watches, perfumes, brandies
for the good life, so cheaply underpriced
that only the crime rate is on the rise
in streets blighted with sun, stone arches
and plazas blown dry by the hysteria
of rumour. A condominium drowns
in vacancy; its bargains are dusted,
but only a jewelled housefly drones
over the bargains. The roulettes spin
rustily to the wind; the vigorous trade
that every morning would begin afresh
by revving up green water round the pierhead
heading for where the banks of silver thresh.

Frederiksted Nights

The goombay band or whatever
combination of Chicano charge
and black funk ignites the fish-fries
by the sizzling pierhead
with the sharks of submarines cruising
like the Puerta Ricenan putas
or lemon Dominican whores
the electric guitars rocketing
at the terrified, empty hotels,
all anger in the groin,
the bomb-cock,
the crotch-trap,
the thudding, explosive pelvis,
to which even the yachts nod,
to which a volley of bullets
sputters under the coalpots,
are gone dead
short-circuited.
The moon is a blown bulb.

And the La Cuenca Café
which only means 'The Corner'
a beastly green, pink and beige
is also out. Closed.
The plastic tablecloths are whipped away,
the defeated Chicano proprietor
gone back to the Main, maybe.
What is remarkable is
that he has taken you with him,

when he served us,
I did not know you would be stolen,
There is nothing around La Cuenca.

There is only the white street,
with the white gates and the oleanders,
and a library full of dead books,
houses, the ochre poorhouse, a hotel,
banks. It is simply another town.
It is simply fish-fry music,
or so I tell myself. Simply.

But my eyes wince at the names of shops
the empty tables are eating my heart;
nothing shines,
your radiance also turned off
by your own hand. So, tonight
when the foolish moon
gapes at the stupid pier,
and the boring music blares

I'll kick its ashes with my foot,
the fishbones, the cold songs,
feel vague as the moon in daylight,
and abhor the cheap green curtains
of the La Cuenca Café.

My life has no corners to turn.
You are young. Go.
I will not turn down any more alleys
to find someone as astonishing;
and in the end, one always
comes to this,
to the dock,
the rain-hazed horizon
and the corpses of poems.

Frederiksted, Dusk

Sunset, the cheapest of all picture-shows,
was all they waited for: old men like empties
set down from morning outside the alms-house,
to let the rising evening brim their eyes,
and, in one row, return the level stare
of light that shares its mortal properties
with the least stone in Frederiksted, as if
more tha. mortality brightened the air,
like a girl tanning on a rock alone
who fills with light. Whatever it is
that leaves bright flesh like sand and turns it chill,
not age alone, they were old, but a state
made possible by their collective will,
would shine in them like something between life
and death, our two concrete simplicities,
and waited too in, seeming not to wait,
substantial light and insubstantial stone.

Sunday Lemons

Desolate lemons, hold
tight, in your bowl of earth,
the light to your bitter flesh,

let a lemon glare
be all your armour
this naked Sunday,

your inflexible light
bounce off the shields of apples
so real, they seem waxen,

share your acid silence
with this woman's remembering
Sundays of other fruit,

till by concentration
you grow, a phalanx of helmets
braced for anything,

hexagonal cities where bees
died purely for sweetness,
your lamps be the last to go

on this polished table
this Sunday, which demands
more than the faith of candles

than helmeted conquistadors

dying like bees, multiplying
memories in her golden head;

as the afternoon vagues
into indigo, let your lamps
hold in this darkening earth

bowl, still life, but a life
beyond tears or the gaieties
of dew, the gay, neon damp

of the evening that blurs
the form of this woman lying,
a lemon, a flameless lamp.

Schloss Erla

Summer lies drugged with prose,
beer-bellied, like Brueghel,
bee-droned. The folk drowse
by the dragonfly-stung pool
where ring on hypnotic ring
widens. The rings will settle,
the air change, and quietly, a chill
flute give every leaf a fatal
edge. Prepare the fall; the fall,
when apples find the subtleties
of autumn sweetest. On the wall
of your New York apartment
you have hung a small summer
picture of Schloss Erla. You fill
and ring your reverie with smoke
around fire-coloured hair.
It is August in Austria.
Castles are lost to a horizon
frail as ash, as far
away as wood-smoke. The zone
that is your sadness rings you,
but sadness is your season
like the apples, as you ripen
to a fullness that can endure
the blazing lie of summer; for,
at the core of passion, you've
always sensed the cold.

The Cloud

And, laterally,
to Adam's pulsing eye,
the erect ridges would throb and recede,

a sigh under the fig tree and a sky
deflating to the serpent's punctured hiss,
repeating you will die.

The woman lay still as the settling mountains.
There was another silence
all was thick with it;

the clouds given a mortal destination,
the silent shudder from the broken branch
where the sap dripped

from the torn tree.
When she, his death,
turned on her side and slept,
the breath he drew was his first real breath.

What left the leaves,
the phosphorescent air
was both God and the serpent leaving him.
Neither could curse or bless.

Pollen was drifting to the woman's hair,
his eye felt brighter,
a cloud's slow shadow slowly covered them,

and, as it moved, he named it Tenderness.

New World

Then after Eden,
was there one surprise?
O yes, the awe of Adam
at the first bead of sweat.

Thenceforth, all flesh
had to be sown with salt,
to feel the edge of seasons,
fear and harvest,
joy, that was difficult,
but was, at least, his own.

The snake? It would not rust
on its forked tree.
The snake admired labour,
it would not leave him alone.

And both would watch the leaves
silver the alder,
oaks yellowing October,
everything turning money,

so when Adam was exiled
to our New Eden, in the ark's gut,
the coined snake coiled there for good
fellowship also; that was willed.

Adam had an idea.
He and the snake would share
the loss of Eden for a profit.
So both made the New World. And it looked good.

Adam's Song

The adulteress stoned to death,
is killed in our own time
by whispers, by the breath
that films her flesh with slime.

The first was Eve,
who horned God for the serpent,
for Adam's sake; which makes
everyone guilty or Eve innocent.

Nothing has changed
for men still sing the song that Adam sang
against the world he lost to vipers,

the song to Eve
against his own damnation;
he sang it in the evening of the world

with the lights coming on in the eyes
of panthers in the peaceable kingdom
and his death coming out of the trees,

he sings it, frightened
of the jealousy of God and at the price
of his own death,

the song ascends to God who wipes his eyes

'Heart, you are in my heart as the bird rises,
heart, you are in my heart while the sun sleeps,
heart, you lie still in me as the dew is,
you weep within me, as the rain weeps.'

Vigil in the Desert

It is from our friends, the hyenas,
with rotting laughter
that, maimed, we have come to choose
the desert dignities of silence,

the dry peace of the anchorite
that whips their parched throats to bark:
barren! Barren!

While, by this runnel
of ferns, we hoard
every syllabic raindrop

where the sky bends
like a bay window
that holds the tiny jewelled head of God

who multiplies in every bead
while round and round and round
the gritted smile of the hermit

circle the evangelical hyenas.

The Brother

That smiler next to you who whispers
brother

knife him.

That man who borrowed your coat
the one of many colours

reclaim it as yours.

Fear your best friends like fire,
it's the cost of this winter,

take him again into your heart's cave

but bind him.

That crippled angel, the Bactrian
who eased your arse out of your own tent,
maim him;

they know when you imitate Christ,
but no man has three cheeks,
and treachery exhausts the patience

even of false saints.
Move from the breath that is soured by envy,
move from those who never have change
but exact thirty pieces of silver

in the name of a cause.
They light a flare in the brain
that cannot let you rest.

And when your love is spent,
in Eden, who sleeps happiest?
The serpent.

Preparing for Exile

Why do I imagine the death of Mandelstam
among the yellowing coconuts,
why does my gift already look over its shoulder
for a shadow to fill the door
and pass this very page into eclipse?
Why does the moon increase into an arc-lamp
and the inkstain on my hand prepare to press thumb-downward
before a shrugging sergeant?
What is this new odour in the air
that was once salt, that smelt like lime at daybreak,
and my cat, I know I imagine it, leap from my path,
and my children's eyes already seem like horizons,
and all my poems, even this one, wish to hide?

Party Night at the Hilton

In our upside-down hotel, in that air-conditioned
roomful of venal, vengeful party-hacks,
lunch-drunk, scotch-drunk, cigar and brandy-stoned,
arguing, insulting till coherence cracks,
poor voice on the rock of power, drained
of every sense but retching indignation
before these pimp Nkrumahs! Their minds
greased by infanticide, generation on generation
heaped in a famine of imagination,
while dacrons sleek their paunches and behinds
with air, hot air. Guilt, sweated
out in glut, while outside, a black wind,
circles the room with jasmine, like a whore's
perfume or second secretary's lotion. Fear those laws
which ex-slaves praise with passion. Pissed, dead
drunk, I soar to hellish light. In the lobby,
cigars with eyes like agents drilling me.

The Lost Federation

You should crawl into rocks away from
the stare of the fisherman,
you, yes, you!

Don't you remember the hustings by the beach
with their sulphurous lanterns,
and your lies in the throat of the sea?

You should get your arse baked till your back
is an old map of blisters,
and your lips crack

like the soil for the water you promised
on the dais, with the sound system
and the sisters calling you Jesus,

and come back with a sieve for your heart,
your brain like a rusted can,
and your bilge reeking,

turn your head, man, I'm speaking
now, I haven't spoken enough, I am speaking
so do what you want, man!

When the first roar came you were astounded,
it was sweeping your heart like a hurricane;
but what are your promises? A grounded

ribbed vessel that the naked
children play through. Listen, you

could still come with me again,
to watch the rain coming from far
like rain, not like votes,

like the ocean, like the wind,
not like an overwhelming majority,
you, who served the people a dung cake of maggots,

that rain cannot extinguish
the processional flambeaux of the poui,
the immortelles, feel it with me

again, you bastard papas,
how it seeps through the pores,
how it loads the sponge of the heart

with the grief of a people,
or smile at this rage, then,
buzzard in a conference coat,

bishop in buzzard's surplice,
crows circling like shadows
over this page,

ministers administering
the last rights to a people,
cabinet, crowded with skeletons,

here's a swinging convocation of bishops
and ministers on the old beach.
Corbeaux. And nobody here with a flashbulb!

Parades, Parades

There's the wide desert, but no one marches
except in the pads of old caravans,
there is the ocean, but the keels incise
the precise, old parallels,
there's the blue sea above the mountains
but they scratch the same lines
in the jet trails,
so the politicians plod
without imagination, circling
the same sombre gardens
with its fountain dry in the forecourt,
the gri-gri palms desicating
dung pods like goats,
the same lines rule the White Papers,
the same steps ascend Whitehall,
and only the name of the fool changes
under the plumed white cork-hat
for the Independence Parades
revolving around, in calypso,
to the brazen joy of the tubas.

Why are the eyes of the beautiful
and unmarked children
in the uniforms of the country
bewildered and shy,
why do they widen in terror
of the pride drummed into their minds?
Were they truer, the old songs,
when the law lived far away,

when the veiled queen, her girth
as comfortable as cushions,
upheld the orb with its stern admonitions?
We wait for the changing of statues,
for the change of parades.

Here he comes now, here he comes!
Papa! Papa! With his crowd,
the sleek, waddling seals of his Cabinet,
trundling up to the dais,
as the wind puts its tail between
the cleft of the mountain, and a wave
coughs once, abruptly.
Who will name this silence
respect? Those forced, hoarse hosannas
awe? That tin-ringing tune
from the pumping, circling horns
the New World? Find a name
for that look on the faces
of the electorate. Tell me
how it all happened, and why
I said nothing.

The Silent Woman

for Jean Miles

'No, not under the vault of another sky,
not under the shelter of other wings.
I was with my people then,
there where my people were doomed to be.'

Anna Akhmatova

Now the executives in business suits,
the dealers in shrugs and smiles
like all the other smilers who have lived
can settle with relief now
to their luncheons, appointments and commissions,
because her final silence has arrived,
until another like her, some woman
or man with the heart of this woman,
some accounts clerk, some public servant, broken
again, by the cost in agony
of public service, speaks. Miss Miles,
it was better to be broken
than like the rest, your betters,
to leave the truth, unspoken.
Come gentlemen, you aren't that busy, come Creon,
come, help Antigone lift up this woman.

Dread Song

Forged from the fire of Exodus
the iron of the tribe,

bright as the lion light, Isaiah,
the anger of the tribe

that the crack must come
and sunder the stone

and the sky-stone fall
on Babylon, Babylon,

the crack in the prison wall
in the chasm of tenements

when the high, high C, Joshua
cry, as I for my tribe:

but in the black markets
lizard-smart poets

selling copper tributes
changing skin with the tribe

and the tribe still buys it
the dreams and the lies

that there'll come to market
as the brethren divide

like the Red Sea to Moses
halt by Aaron's rod

the rod which is both serpent
and staff of brotherhood

more cripples like questions
on the snakes of black tires

Solomon in black glasses
hiding his eyes

shaking hands all round
statistics and jiving

to the clapping of the tribe;
Economics and Exodus,

embrace us within
bracket and parenthesis

their snake arms of brotherhood
(the brackets of the bribe)

Want to open your mouth, then?
Shake your dread locks, brethren?

and see one door yawn wide,
then the lion-den of prison,

sky mortar like stone;
Brothers in Babylon, Doc! Uncle! Papa!

Behind the dark glasses
the fire is dying

the coal of my people;
no vision, no flame,

no deepness, no danger,
more music, less anger

more sorrow, less shame
more talk of the River

that wash out my name
let things be the same

forever and ever
the faith of my tribe.

The Dream

I stood on the sand, I saw
black horsemen galloping towards
me, they were all white like
the waves and turbanned too
like the breakers, their flags
thinning away into spume; white,
white were their snorting horses.
I saw them. It was no dream. They
rode through me, they came from
my home, as fresh as the waves
and older than this sea.
Rider and breaker, one cry!
I have seen them at a ceremony
of lances, white-robed knights,
(I forget the names of our tribes).
They are coming, I trembled, to claim
their brothers, to bring them
home, thundering round the edge
of the headland, exploding from sight!
Spears shoot on the edge
of the wave every moonlit night —
The horsemen will keep their pledge,
the knights of Bornu.

Natural History
I
The Walking Fish

There was a shape across the bay,
stunned on the sand.
It was like a huge fish, or a man
like a huge fish.

It did not move. I could not look away.
It was here I began.
The waves

scudded over my back;
where they snagged they formed scales
scalloped at the edges. My ducts
subside now. Bellows.

For years
my sky has been water;
I have paddled under the bubbles
of phosphorescent moons,

my eyes
glazed by a film
that set into gelatinous scales,
their quick salt itch drying.

The scallops
harden, the nostrils shrivel,
splayed, the webbed fingers burrow
into this sand.

I'll wait.
Waves, waves wash over my back.
The tears prickle quickly out of my eye.

I'll wait
for a geological epoch
My biggest thrill is a blink
One blink every geological epoch.

The waves now
have receded into the far, faint
caves of my ears. I shed glazed
fins like sea-fans, dragon-serrated.

This beach,
is just like the other where I was born.
I feel green and black with a chain-mail
of silver, then a fine net of pores

through which the sea breathes
through which the Atlantic remembers,
through which in flutes the five oceans whistle

Lumber once, then
stop. Dragons no longer fly,
the groaning mastodon's gone down

in the brea of muck
the tiger's sabres turned coral,
the pterodactyl shrunk to a bat,

but I name
this foothold with a grateful croak,
earth. I can arch my back

I can squat,

I can paddle my forefins,
fingers of grass in the sand
and grass in my fingers

Lurch up.
Earth falls away. Up.
The horizon drops past my belly.

Dunes, there,
behind the dunes, others,
my kind, other gutturals waiting,

learning
their unsteady walk.
There is nothing in that ocean
above the horizon,

in that sea,
where the great white fish swam,
everything has changed

or has changed us.
Or, as I
paddle this air, breathe this new sea, am I
still swimming through one gigantic eye?

II
Frogs

Moonlight, and the sun-dials of frogs sadden the lawn.
Tires will grind them like head-lamp marbled crabs, like splayed
Biafran children, and tomorrow's sun
reprint them till they take on
the monochrome of asphalt
the tabloid, iron tones of death. History

is natural; famine, genocide,
as natural as moonlight,
and man is great who rises at this cost;
like the Bikini turtles, who, after the holocaust
swam deeper into sand, their history reversed
from nature, or the mad birds
that burrowed into earth, while ocean,
a god once, rages, at a loss for words.

III
Turtles

To have misplaced your instinct for the sea,
to blunder with each cataracted eye
staring past panic, or panic so bland,
the gripping, slipping paddles row through sand
changed by man's will to ocean.
The mutant turtles teach adaptability
to man, the walking fish,
who with his forefins used to pray upright,
before the bomb's fountaining: 'Let there be light!'

IV
Butterflies

They fall in ribbons down the paths of ocean,
the foam-pale butterflies, but the flowers are salt.
They prove the charms of rapine, that the emotion
called beauty has earned this result.

Names

for Edward Brathwaite

I

My race began as the sea began,
with no nouns, and with no horizon,
with pebbles under my tongue,
with a different fix on the stars.

But now my race is here,
in the sad oil of Levantine eyes,
in the flags of the Indian fields,

I began with no memory,
I began with no future,
but I looked for that moment
when the mind was halved by a horizon,

I have never found that moment
when the mind was halved by a horizon
for the goldsmith from Benares,
the stone-cutter from Canton,
as a fishline sinks, the horizon
sinks in the memory.

Have we melted into a mirror,
leaving our souls behind?
The goldsmith from Benares,
the stone-cutter from Canton,
the bronzesmith from Benin.

A sea-eagle screams from the rock,
and my race began like the osprey

with that cry,
that terrible vowel,
that I!

Behind us all the sky folded,
as history folds over a fishline,
and the foam foreclosed
with nothing in our hands

but this stick
to trace our names on the sand
which the sea erased again, to our indifference.

II

And when they named these bays
bays,
was it nostalgia or irony?

In the uncombed forest,
in uncultivated grass
where was there elegance
except in their mockery?
Where were the courts of Castille,
Versailles' colonnades
supplanted by cabbage palms
with Corinthian crests,
belittling diminutives,
then, little Versailles
meant plans for a pigsty,
names for the sour apples
and green grapes
of their exile.

Their memory turned acid
but the names held,
Valencia glows
with the lanterns of oranges,
Mayaro's
charred candelabra of cocoa.
Being men, they could not live
except they first presumed
the right of every thing to be a noun.
The African acquiesced,
repeated, and changed them

Listen, my children, say:
moubain: the hogplum,
cerise: the wild cherry,
baie-la: the bay,
with the fresh green voices
they were once themselves
in the way the wind bends
our natural inflections.

These palms are greater than Versailles,
for no man made them,
their fallen columns greater than Castille,
no man unmade them
except the worm, who has no helmet,
but was always the emperor,

and children, look at these stars
over Valencia's forest!

Not Orion,
not Betelgeuse,
tell me, what do they look like?
Answer, you damned little Arabs!
Sir, fireflies caught in molasses.

Sainte Lucie

I
The Villages

Laborie, Choiseul, Vieuxfort, Dennery,
from these sun-bleached villages
where the church-bell caves in the sides
of one grey-scurfed shack that is shuttered
with warped boards, with rust
with crabs crawling under the house-shadow
where the children played house;
a net rotting among cans, the sea-net
of sunlight trolling the shallows
catching nothing all afternoon,
from these I am growing no nearer
to what secret eluded the children
· under the house-shade, in the far bell, the noon's
stunned amethystine sea,
something always being missed
between the floating shadow and the pelican
in the smoke from over the next bay
in that shack on the lip of the sandpit
whatever the seagulls cried out for
with the grey drifting ladders of rain
and the great grey tree of the waterspout,
for which the dolphins kept diving, that
should have rounded the day.

II

Pomme arac,
otaheite apple,
pomme cythere,

pomme granate,
moubain,
z'ananas
the pine apple's
Aztec helmet,
pomme,
I have forgotten
what pomme for
the Irish potato,
cerise,
the cherry,
z'aman
sea-almonds
by the crisp
sea-bursts,
au bord de la 'ouviere.
Come back to me
my language.
Come back,
cacao,
grigri,
solitaire,
ciseau
the scissor-bird
no nightingales
except, once,
in the indigo mountains
of Jamaica, blue depth,
deep as coffee,
flicker of pimento,
the shaft light
on a yellow ackee
the bark alone bare

jardins
en montagnes

en haut betassion
the wet leather reek
of the hill donkey

evening opens at
a text of fireflies,
in the mountain huts
ti cailles betassion
candles,
candleflies
the black night bending
cups in its hard palms
cool thin water
this is important water,
important?
imported?
water is important
also very important
the red rust drum
the evening deep
as coffee
the morning powerful
important coffee
the villages shut
all day in the sun.

In the empty schoolyard
teacher dead today
the fruit rotting
yellow on the ground,
dyes from Gauguin
the pomme arac dyes
the earth purple,
the ochre roads
still waiting in the sun
for my shadow,

O so you is Walcott?
you is Roddy brother?
Teacher Alix son?
and the small rivers
with important names.

And the important corporal
in the country station
en betassion
looking towards the thick
green slopes of cocoa
the sun that melts
the asphalt at noon,
and the woman in the shade
of the breadfruit bent over
the lip of the valley,
below her, blue-green
the lost, lost valleys
of sugar, the bus-rides,
the fields of bananas
the tanker still rusts
in the lagoon at Roseau,
and around what corner

was uttered a single
yellow leaf,
from the frangipani
a tough bark, reticent,
but when it flowers
delivers hard lilies,
pungent, recalling
Martina, or Eunice
or Lucilla,
who comes down the steps
with the cool, side flow
as spring water eases

over shelves of rock
in some green ferny hole
by the road in the mountains,
her smile like the whole country
her smell, earth,
red-brown earth, her armpits
a reaping, her arms
saplings, an old woman
that she is now,
with other generations
of daughters flowing
down the steps,
gens betassion,
belle ti fille betassion,
until their teeth go,
and all the rest,

O Martinas, Lucillas,
I'm a wild golden apple
that will burst with love,
of you and your men,
those I never told enough
with my young poet's eyes
crazy with the country,
generations going,
generations gone,
moi c'est gens St Lucie.
C'est la moi sorti;
is there that I born.

Iona: Mabouya Valley

(Saint Lucian *conte* or narrative song, heard on the back
of an open truck travelling to Vieûxfort, some years ago)

Ma Kilman, Bon Dieu kai punir 'ous,
Pour qui raison parcequi' ous entrer trop religion.
Oui, l'autre cote, Bon Dieu kai benir 'ous,
Bon Dieu kai benir 'ous parcequi 'ous faire charite l'argent.
Corbeau aille Curacao, i' voyait l'argent ba 'ous,
Ous prend l'argent cela
Ous mettait lui en cabaret.
Ous pas ka lire, ecrire, 'ous pas ka parler Anglais,
Ous tait supposer ca; cabaret pas ni benefice.
L'heure Corbeau devirait,
L'tait ni, I' tait ni l'argent,
L'heure i' rivait ici,
Oui, maman! Corbeau kai fou!

Iona dit Corbeau, pendant 'ous tait Curacao,
Moi fait deux 'tits mamaille, venir garder si c'est ca 'ous,
Corbeau criait 'Mama! Bon soir, messieurs, mesdames,
Lumer lampe-la ba mwen
Pour moi garder ces mamailles-la!'
Corbeau virait dire: 'Moi save toutes negres ka semble,
I peut si pas ca moin,
Moi kai soigner ces mamailles-la!'

Oui, Corbeau partit, Corbeau descend Roseau,
Allait chercher travail, pourqui 'peut soigner ces mamailles-la,
Iona dit Corbeau pas tait descendre Roseau,
Mais i' descend Roseau, jamettes Rosseau tomber derriere-i'

Phillipe Mago achetait un sax bai Corbeau,
I' pas ni temps jouer sax-la,
Sax-man comme lui prendre la vie-lui.

Samedi bon matin, Corbeau partit descendre en ville,
Samedi apres-midi, nous 'tendre la mort Corbeau.
Ca fait moi la peine; oui, ca brulait coeur-moin,
Ca penetrait moin, l'heure moin 'tendre la mort Corbeau.

Iona dit comme-ca: ca qui fait lui la peine,
Ca qui brulait coeur-lui: saxophone Corbeau pas jouer.
Moin 'tendre un corne cornait
a sur bord roseaux-a,
Moi dit: 'Doux-doux, moin kai chercher volants ba 'ous'
L'heure moin 'rivait la, moin fait raconte epi Corbeau,
I' dit: 'Corne-la qui cornait-a,
c'est Iona ka cornait moin.'

Guitar-man la ka dire:
'Nous tous les deux c'est guitar-man,
Pas prendre ca pour un rien,
C'est meme beat-la nous ka chember.'

Iona mariee, Dimanche a quatre heures.
Mardi, a huit heures, i' aille l'hopital.
I'fait un bombe, mari-lui cassait bras-lui.
L'heure moi joindre maman-ous,
Moin kai conter toute ca 'ous 'ja faire moin.
Iona!
(N'ai dit maman-ous!)
Iona!
(Ous pas ka 'couter moin!)
Trois jours, trois nuits
Iona bouillit, Iona pas chuitte.
(N'ai dit maman-i' ca)
Toute moune ka dit Iona tourner,

C'est pas tourner Iona tourner, mauvais i' mauvais,
Iona!

IV
Iona: Mabouya Valley
for Eric Branford

Ma Kilman God will punish you,
for the reason that you've got too much religion,
on the other hand, God will bless you,
God will bless you because of your charity.

Corbeau went to Curacao
He sent you money back
You took the same money
and put it in a rum-shop
You can't read, you can't write, you can't speak English,
You should know that rum-shops make no profit,
When Corbeau come back
He had, yes he had money
when he arrived back here,
Yes Mama, Corbeau'll go crazy.

Iona told Corbeau while you were in Curacao
I made two little children, come and see if they're yours.
Corbeau cried out, 'Mama, Goodnight ladies and gentlemen
Light the lamp there for me
For me to look at these kids,'
Corbeau came back and said 'I know niggers resemble,
They may or may not be mine,
I'll mind them all the same.'

Ah yes, Corbeau then left, he went down to Roseau,

He went to look for work, to mind the two little ones,
Iona told Corbeau, don't go down to Roseau
But he went to Roseau, and Roseau's whores fell on him.
Phillipe Mago, brought Corbeau a saxophone,
He had no time to play the sax
A saxman just like him took away his living.

Saturday morning early, Corbeau goes into town.
Saturday afternoon we hear Corbeau is dead.
That really made me sad, that really burnt my heart;
That really went through me when I heard Corbeau was dead.

Iona said like this: it made her sorry too,
It really burnt her heart, that the saxophone will never play.

I heard a horn blowing
by the river reeds down there
Sweetheart, I said, I'll go looking
for flying fish for you.
When I got there, I came across Corbeau
He said that horn you heard
was Iona horning me.

The guitar man's saying
We both are guitar men,
Don't take it for anything,
We both holding the same beat.

Iona got married, Sunday at four o'clock.
Tuesday, by eight o'clock, she's in the hospital.
She made a fare, her husband broke her arm,
when I meet your mother I'll tell what you did me.
Iona,
(I'll tell your maman)
Iona
(You don't listen to me)

Three days and three nights
(Iona boiled, she's still not cooked)
(I'll tell her mother that)
They say Iona's changed
It isn't changed Iona's changed
she's wicked, wicked, that's all
Iona.

V
For the Altar-piece of the Roseau Valley Church, Saint Lucia

I

The chapel, as the pivot of this valley,
round which whatever is rooted loosely turns
men, women, ditches, the revolving fields
of bananas, the secondary roads,
draws all to it, to the altar
and the massive altar-piece;
like a dull mirror, life
repeated there,
the common life outside
and the other life it holds
a good man made it.

Two earth-brown labourers
dance the botay in it, the drum sounds under
the earth, the heavy foot.

                    This is a rich valley,
It is fat with things.

Its roads radiate like aisles from the altar towards
those acres of bananas, towards
leaf-crowded mountains
rain-bellied clouds
in haze, in iron heat;

This is a cursed valley,
ask the broken mules, the swollen children,
ask the dried women, their gap-toothed men,
ask the parish priest, who, in the altar-piece
carries a replica of the church,
ask the two who could be Eve and Adam dancing.

II

Five centuries ago
in the time of Giotto
this altar might have had
in one corner, when God was young
ST OMER ME FECIT AETAT whatever his own age now,
GLORIA DEI and to God's Mother also.

It is signed with music.
It turns the whole island.
You have to imagine it empty on a Sunday afternoon
between adorations

Nobody can see it and it is there,
nobody adores the two who could be Eve and Adam dancing.

A Sunday at three o'clock
when the real Adam and Eve have coupled
and lie in re-christening sweat

his sweat on her still breasts,
her sweat on his panelled torso

that hefts bananas
that has killed snakes
that has climbed out of rivers,

now, as on the furred tops of the hills
a breeze moving the hairs on his chest

on a Sunday at three o'clock
when the snake pours itself
into a chalice of leaves.

The sugar factory is empty.

Nobody picks bananas,
no trucks raising dust on their way to Vieuxfort,
no helicopter spraying

the mosquito's banjo, yes,
and the gnat's violin, okay,

okay, not absolute Adamic silence,
the valley of Roseau is not the Garden of Eden,
and those who inhabit it, are not in heaven,

so there are little wires of music
some marron up in the hills, by AuxLyons,
some christening.

A boy banging a tin by the river,
with the river trying to sleep.
But nothing can break that silence,

which comes from the depth of the world,
from whatever one man believes he knows of God
and the suffering of his kind,

it comes from the wall of the altar-piece
ST OMER AD GLORIAM DEI FECIT
in whatever year of his suffering.

III

After so many bottles of white rum in a pile,
after the flight of so many little fishes
from the brush that is the finger of St Francis,

after the deaths
of as many names as you want,
Iona, Julian, Ti-Nomme, Cacao,
like the death of the cane-crop in Roseau Valley, St Lucia.

After five thousand novenas
and the idea of the Virgin
coming and going like a little lamp

after all that,
your faith like a canoe at evening coming in,
like a relative who is tired of America,
like a woman coming back to your house

that sang in the ropes of your wrist
when you lifted this up;
so that, from time to time, on Sundays

between adorations, one might see,
if one were there, and not there,
looking in at the windows

the real faces of angels.

Over Colorado

When Whitman's beard unrolled like the Pacific,
when he quit talking
to prophesy the great waggons

the dream began to lumber to delirium.
Once, flying over Colorado
its starved palomino mountains

I saw, like ants, a staggering file
of Indians enter a cloud's beard;
then the cloud broke on

a frozen brave, his fossil
a fern-print on the spine of rock,
his snow-soft whisper

Colorado, rust and white;
the snow his praise, the snow
his obliterator.

That was years ago,
in a jet crossing to Los Angeles,
I don't know why it comes now,

or why I see only this
through those democratic vistas
parting your leaves of grass.

Spring Street in '58

for Frank O'Hara

Dirt under the fingernails of the window-ledge,
in the rococo ceiling, grime
flowering like a street opera.
Ah candles, Con-Edison nights
in the packing-case district
of my little Italy,
ah, my blown-out,
fly-blown Bohemia!

There was dirt on the peach tan
of the girls of the gold Mid-West,
ou sont ces vierges?
Ah, Frank, elles sont
aux Spring Falls, Iowa,
Columbus, Tucson,
gone with coarse ponytails, gone
with autumnal reveries of Indian blankets,
birches, and the snow creek on the calendar
quivering its palomino hide
to the housefly; back
to the picket fences, Minnesota,
to the strict elms that predicted their return,
to the flowered headscarves and the supermarkets
with the Evergreen Reviews they cannot burn.

And the cheap cocktail bars
by which I homed,
their neon flickered like Mars,
then, we could still write 'The moon . . .'

nostalgia was halvah and nougat
and was out of fashion, like death;
and one caught style from others like a cold,
and I could look at Mimi washing her soiled feet
as life imitating Lautrec.

In Spring Street's dirty hermitage, where I
crouched over poems, and drawings, I
knew we'd all live as long as Hokusai.

Ohio, Winter

for James Wright

It's your country, Jim, and what
I imagine there may not exist:
summer grass clutching derailed freight
trains till they rust
and blacken like buffalo.
This winter is white as wheat
and width is its terror, you're
right; behind the clenched, white
barns all afternoon the night
hides with a knife; the road
grovels under a blizzard,
frost glazes the eyelid
of the windscreen, and every barn or
farm-light goes lonelier, lonelier.

For Pablo Neruda

I am not walking on sand,
but I feel I am walking on sand,
this poem is accompanying me on sand.
Fungus lacing the rock,
on the ribs, mould. Moss
feathering the mute roar
of the staved in throat
of the wreck, the crab gripping.

Why this loop of correspondences,
as your voice grows hoarser
than the chafed Pacific? Your voice
falling soundless as snow on
the petrified Andes, the snow
like feathers from the tilting
rudderless condors,
emissary in a black suit, who
walks among eagles, hand, whose
five knuckled peninsula
bars the heartbreaking ocean?

Hear the ambassador of velvet
open the felt-hinged door,
the black flag flaps toothless
over Isla Negra. You said
when others like me despaired:
climb the moss-throated stairs
to the crest of Macchu Picchu,
break your teeth like a pick on

the obdurate, mottled terraces,
wear the wind, soaked with rain
like a cloak, above absences,

and for us, in the New World,
our older world, you become
a benign, rigorous uncle,
and through you we fanned open
to others, to the sand-rasped
mutter of César Vallejo, to
the radiant, self-circling
sunstone of Octavio, men
who, unlike the Saxons, I am tempted
to call by their Christian names

we were all netted to one rock
by vines of iron, our livers
picked by corbeaux and condors
in the New World, in a new word
brotherhood, word which arrests
the crests of the snowblowing ocean
in its flash to a sea of sierras,
the round fish mouths of our children
the word *cantan.* All this
you have done for me. Gracias.

Volcano

Joyce was afraid of thunder,
but lions roared at his funeral
from the Zurich zoo.
Was it Zurich or Trieste?
No matter. These are legends, as much
as the death of Joyce is a legend,
or the strong rumour that Conrad
is dead, and that VICTORY is ironic,
On the edge of the night-horizon
from this beach house on the cliffs
there are now, till dawn,
two glares from the miles-out
at sea derricks; they are like
the glow of the cigar
and the glow of the volcano
at VICTORY'S end.
One could abandon writing
for the slow-burning signals
of the great, to be, instead
their ideal reader, ruminative,
voracious, making the love of masterpieces
superior to attempting
to repeat or outdo them,
and be the greatest reader in the world.
At least it requires awe,
which has been lost to our time,
so many people have seen everything,
so many people can predict,
so many refuse to enter the silence

of victory, the indolence
that burns at the core,
so many are no more than
erect ash, like the cigar,
so many take thunder for granted.
How common is the lightning,
how lost the leviathans
we no longer look for!
There were giants in those days.
In those days they made good cigars.
I must read more carefully.

The Wind in the Dooryard

for Eric Roach

I didn't want this poem to come
from the torn mouth,
I didn't want this poem to come
from his salt body,

but I will tell you what he celebrated:

He writes of the wall with spilling coralita
from the rim of the rich garden,
and the clean dirt yard
clean as the parlour table
with a yellow tree
an ackee, an almond
a pomegranate
in the clear vase of sunlight,

sometimes he put his finger
on the pulse of the wind,
when he heard the sea in the cedars.
He went swimming to Africa,
but he felt tired,
he chose that way
to reach his ancestors.

No, I did not want to write this,
but, doesn't the sunrise
force itself through the curtain
of the trembling eyelids?
When the cows are statues in the misting field

that sweats out the dew,
and the horse lifts its iron head
and the jaws of the sugar mules
ruminate and grind like the factory?

I did not want to hear it again,
the echo of broken windmills,
the mutter of the wild yams creeping
over the broken palings,
the noise of the moss
stitching the stone baracoons,

but the rain breaks
on the foreheads of the wild yams,
the dooryard opens the voice
of his rusty theme,
and the first quick drops of the drizzle
the libations to Shango
dry fast as sweat on the forehead
and our tears also.

The peasant reeks sweetly of bush,
he smells the same as his donkey
they smell of the high, high country
of clouds and stunted pine,
the man wipes his hand
that is large as a yam
and as crusty with dirt
across the tobacco-stained
paling stumps of his torn mouth,
he rinses with the mountain dew,
and he spits out pity.

I did not want it to come,
but sometimes, under the armpit
of the hot sky over the country

the wind smells of salt
and a certain breeze lifts
the sprigs of the coralita
as if, like us,
lifting our heads, at our happiest,
it too smells the freshness of life.

The Chelsea

I

Nothing, not the hotel's beige dankness, not
the neon-flickered drifts of dirty rain,
the marigolds' drying fire from their pot
above a dead fireplace, mean ruin
anymore to him. The mirror's reflexes
are nerveless and indifferent as he is
to fame and money. He will find success
in the lost art of failure, so he says
to the flawless girl framed in the mirror's tarnish.
She's more than the hotel's bronze plaque of greats
who hit the bottle or the street, grew rich
or famous. Their fame curls like layers of beige
paint, just as those mirrored flowers will die.
The clear-eyed girl letting cold tap-water
run on, watches herself watching him lie.

II

Between the darkening drapes of the hotel
We'd watch the lion-coloured twilight come
stalking up the sandstone, tall
bluff of the West Side Gymnasium,
the wide sky yawning as the tame light curled
around Manhattan, then felt the room fill
with a vague pity, as its objects furred
to indistinction, chair, bed, desk, turn soft
as drowsing lions. Love gives a selfish strength
if lonely lives, down the stale corridors,
still, as they turn the key, nod down the length

of their whole life at slowly-closing doors,
In other's hell we made our happiness.
Across the window furnished room and loft
lamplit their intimacies. Happier lives,
settled in ruts, and great for wanting less.

The Bridge

Good-evening, here is the news.
Tonight here, in Manhattan, on a bridge,
a matter that began

two years ago between this man
and the woman next to him, is ending.
And that concludes the news for tonight,

except the old news of the river's fairy light,
and the bridge lit up
like the postcards, the cliché views,

except that they have nothing to grip the bridge with,
and across the river all the offices are on
for safety, they are like over-typed carbon

held up to light with the tears showing.
The heart, that is girded iron melts. The iron
bridge is an empty party. A man a feather.

There are too many lights on.
It's far too fanciful; that's all;
the iron rainbow to the bright water bending.

Neither is capable of going
they stand like still beasts in a hunter's moon,
silent like beasts, but soon,

the woman
will sense in her eyes dawn's rain beginning,
and the man

feel in his muscles the river's startled flowing.

Endings

Things do not explode
they fail, they fade,

as sunlight fades from the flesh
as the foam drains quick in the sand,

even love's lightning flash
has no thunderous end,

it dies with the sound
of flowers fading like the flesh

from sweating pumice stone,
everything shapes this

till we are left
with the silence that surrounds Beethoven's head.

California

Heal me, valley.
The gull
names Santa Barbara.

Green trough
of between mountains
through which a single
pigeon sails,

the hill-crest held
on the edge of its plunge
the wave
before it breaks down

and, in profile
against the curved green
breaker of forest

the ease-bringing
dove.

The Fist

The fist clenched round my heart
loosens a little, and I gasp
brightness; but it tightens
again. When have I ever not loved
the pain of love? But this has moved

past love to mania. This has the strong
clench of the madman, this is
gripping the ledge of unreason, before
plunging howling into the abyss.

Hold hard then, heart. This way at least you live.

Love After Love

The time will come
when, with elation,
you will greet yourself arriving
at your own door, in your own mirror,
and each will smile at the other's welcome,

and say sit here. Eat.
You will love again the stranger who was your self,
Give wine. Give bread. Give back your heart
to itself, to the stranger who has loved you

all your life, whom you ignored
for another, who knows you by heart.
Take down the love-letters from the bookshelf

the photographs, the desperate notes,
peel your own image from the mirror.
Sit. Feast on your life.

Midsummer, England

At Henley, the sky-blue striped pavilions
are boat-houses, the royal river
beer-bottle green with broken lights,
the legendary landscapes are alive,
palpable air; woods, castles, manors, suns,
pressing their postcards on you as you drive.

Great summer takes its ease,
ankling the shallows, cloudy dresses bloat
and cling clearly round the women's knees,
as Christ harangues the indifferent from his boat
by Cookham's river.

Riots of colour in the Supplements,
startling bright mustard squares
flare tropically up amid
fields trimmed by centuries of reticence;
midsummer's broad abandon will subside
like hills rolling in heat waves; what will not,
is the fear of darkness entering England's vein,
the noble monuments pissed on by rain,
the imperial blood corrupted, the dark tide.

But summer persists through the pain,
it forces the leaf
and tries, through love-nourishing rain
to dissolve individual grief,
history and heart-break.

Prodigious summer whose black fruit includes,
past this and that great house,
between hills bracketing thunder,
a great cloud's shadow that grows close
as the past, a chill that intrudes
under the heat, under the centuries;
rooks swinging in the wind, under great boughs,
lynched crows, on a green field.

What hurts most is to think that I was healed.

The Bright Field

My nerves steeled against the power of London,
I hurried home that evening, with the sense
we all have, of the crowd's hypocrisy,
to feel my rage, turned on in self-defence,
bear mercy for the anonymity
of every self humbled by massive places,
and I, who moved against a bitter sea,
was moved by the light on Underground-bound faces.

Their sun that would not set was going down
on their flushed faces, brickwork like a kiln,
on pillar-box bright buses between trees,
with the compassion of calendar art;
like walking sheaves of harvest, the quick crowd
thickened in separate blades of cane or wheat
from factories and office doors conveyed
to one end by the loud belt of the street.
And that end brings its sadness, going in
by Underground, by cab, by bullock-cart,
and lances us with punctual, maudlin
pity down lanes or cane-fields, till the heart,
seeing, like dark canes, the river-spires sharpen,
feels an involuntary bell begin
to toll for everything, even in London,
heart of our history, original sin.

The vision that brought Samuel Palmer peace,
that stoked Blake's fury at her furnaces,
flashes from doormen's buttons and the rocks

around Balandra. These slow belfry-strokes
cast in the pool of London, from which swallows
rise in wide rings, and from their bright field, rooks,
mark the same beat by which a pelican goes
across Salybia as the tide lowers.

Dark August

So much rain, so much life like the swollen sky
of this black August. My sister, the sun,
broods in her yellow room and won't come out.

Everything goes to hell; the mountains fume
like a kettle, rivers over-run, still,
she will not rise and turn off the rain.

She's in her room, fondling old things,
my poems, turning her album. Even if thunder falls
like a crash of plates from the sky,

she does not come out.
Don't you know I love you but am hopeless
at fixing the rain? But I am learning slowly

to love the dark days, the steaming hills,
the air with gossiping mosquitoes,
and to sip the medicine of bitterness,

so that when you emerge, my sister,
parting the beads of the rain,
with your forehead of flowers and eyes of forgiveness,

all will not be as it was, but it will be true,
(you see they will not let me love
as I want), because my sister, then

I would have learnt to love black days like bright ones,
the black rain, the white hills, when once
I loved only my happiness and you.

Sea Canes

Half my friends are dead.
I will make you new ones, said earth,
No, give me them back, as they were, instead
with faults and all, I cried.

Tonight I can snatch their talk
from the faint surf's drone,
through the canes, but I cannot walk

on the moonlit leaves of ocean
down that white road alone,
or float with the dreaming motion

of owls leaving earth's load.
O earth, the number of friends you keep
exceeds those left to be loved.

The sea-canes by the cliff flash green and silver
they were the seraph lances of my faith,
but out of what is lost grows something stronger

that has the rational radiance of stone,
enduring moonlight, further than despair,
strong as the wind, that through dividing canes

brings those we love before us, as they were,
with faults and all, not nobler, just there.

The Harvest

If they ask what my favourite flower was,
there's one thing that you'll have to understand:
I learnt to love it by the usual ways
of those who swore to serve truth with one hand,
and one behind their back for cash or praise,
that I surrendered dreaming how I'd stand
in the rewarding autumn of my life,
just ankle-deep in money, thick as leaves,
to bring my poetry, poor, faithful wife
past her accustomed style, well, all the same,
though there's no autumn, nature played the game
with me each fiscal year, when the gold pouis
would guiltily start scattering largesse
like Christian bankers or wind-shook-down thieves.
What I soon learnt was they had changed the script,
left out the golden fall and turned to winter,
to some grey monochrome, much like this metre,
with no gold in it. So, I saw my toil
as a seedy little yard of scrub and root
that gripped for good, and what took in that soil,
was the cheap flower that you see at my foot,
the coarsest, commonest, toughest, nondescript,
resilient violet with its white spot centre.

Midsummer, Tobago

Broad sun-stoned beaches.

White heat.
A green river.

A bridge,
scorched yellow palms

from the summer-sleeping house
drowsing through August.

Days I have held,
days I have lost,

days that outgrow, like daughters,
my harbouring arms.

Force

Life will keep hammering the grass blades into the ground.

I admire this violence;
love is iron. I admire

the brutal exchange between breaker and rock.
They have an understanding.

I may even understand the contract
between the galloping lion and the stunned doe,
there is some yes to terror in her eyes

what I will never understand
is the beast who writes this
and claims the centre of life.

Oddjob, a Bull Terrier

You prepare for one sorrow,
but another comes.
It is not like the weather,
you cannot brace yourself,
the unreadiness is all.
Your companion, the woman,
the friend next to you,
the child at your side,
and the dog,
we tremble for them,
we look sea-ward and muse
it will rain.
We shall get ready for rain,
you do not connect
the sunlight altering
the darkening oleanders
in the sea-garden,
the gold going out of the palms.
You do not connect this
the fleck of the drizzle
on your flesh
with the dog's whimper,
the thunder doesn't frighten,
the readiness is all,
what follows at your feet
is trying to tell you
the silence is all
it is deeper than the readiness,
it is sea-deep,

earth-deep,
love-deep.

The silence
is stronger than thunder,
we are stricken dumb and deep
as the animals who never utter love
as we do, except
it becomes unutterable
and must be said,
in a whimper,
in tears,
in the drizzle that comes to our eyes
not uttering the loved thing's name,
the silence of the dead,
the silence of the deepest buried love is
the one silence,
and whether we bear it for beast,
for child, for woman, or friend,
it is the one love, it is the same,
and it is blest
deepest by loss
it is blest, it is blest.

Earth

Let the day grow on you upward
through your feet
the vegetal knuckles

to your knees of stone,
until by evening you are a black tree;
feel, with evening,

the swifts thicken your hair,
the new moon rising out of your forehead,
and the moonlit veins of silver

running from your armpits
like rivulets under white leaves.
Sleep, as ants

cross over your eyelids.
You have never possessed anything
as deeply as this.

This is all you have owned
from the first outcry
through forever;

you can never be dispossessed.

At Last

To the exiled novelists

You spit on your people,
your people applaud,
your former oppressors
laurel you.
The thorns biting your forehead
are contempt
disguised as concern,
still, you can come home, now.
Before, in your finical gut
the bowels of compassion
petrify to a gallstone,
and your ink deliquesces
into bile. In your eye
every child is born crippled,
every endeavour
is that of the baboon,
can you hear the achievement
of this chimpanzee typing?

We are through with that pastoral
of palm-splashed zebras
soundlessly circling
nostalgic veldts,
with the caved-in balafong
and the snapped strings
of savannah grass,
let your fur-shrouded
Aryan horseman
melt into the snowstorm,

till the page is again
blank, and, under the snowdrift
of the white page, of the white
ocean, all is buried,
generations, generations.

The snows have hardened,
the page is cold, it is glazed
like the snow-lashed eyes
and the freaked, parted mouths
of your horsemen, like the dice
of skulls rolling under
the tilting sea-floor.
Generations, generations,
they did not cross for us to abhor
them, they did not all die
for your prose, those who
perished in the snows or
under the snow-torn billows,

nor do they need to forgive
their children who tear
at the scabs of their names.
We have passed through the fever,
when we heard our voices
when the bells of the anopheles
were ringing in the ears
over the rice-fields,
over the sea-canes
when the morning sunlight
shivered with malaria,
and the night sea grew tepid
with weeds, like a bush-bath.

We have sweated cold sweat
remembering generations,

while you, who have risen
from their sweat-soaked capra
from the tangled night-bed
folded over like snowdrifts
should know that the sun
is no longer ill,
an orange infested with ants,
that this landscape was never
forgiven or forgiving,
while the pelican beats
to the rock of Soledad
to a beat which is neither
poetry nor prose.

I have sweated it out,
generations, generations,
I am growing hoarse
from repeating the praise
of the ape and the ass,
the enslaved, the indentured,
who are nothing. Grass, then
dung. Paths for the good
to walk over. Men.

And now, let it come to fruit,
let me be sure it has flowered
to break from the bitterest root
and the earth that soured,
the flower bursts out of my heart,
the cleft in the rock, at last
flowers, the heart-breaking past
unforgiven and unforgiving,
the net of my veins I have cast
here flashes with living
silver at last, at last!

Winding Up

I live on the water,
alone. Without wife and children.
I have circled every possibility
to come to this:

a low house by grey water,
with windows always open
to the stale sea. We do not choose such things,

but we are what we have made.
We suffer, the years pass,
we shed freight but not our need

for encumbrances. Love is a stone
that settled on the sea-bed
under grey water. Now, I require nothing

from poetry, but true feeling,
no pity, no fame, no healing. Silent wife,
we can sit watching grey water,

and in a life awash
with mediocrity and trash
live rock-like.

I shall unlearn feeling,
unlearn my gift. That is greater
and harder than what passes there for life.

The Morning Moon

Still haunted by the cycle of the moon
racing full sail
past the crouched whale's back of Morne Coco mountain,

I gasp at her sane brightness.

It's early December,
the breeze freshens the skin of this earth,
the goose-skin of water,

and I notice the blue plunge
of shadows down Morne Coco mountain,
December's sun-dial,

happy that the earth is still changing
that the full moon can blind me with her forehead
this bright foreday morning,

and that fine sprigs of white are springing from my beard.

To Return to the Trees

for John Figueroa

Senex, an oak.
Senex, this old sea-almond
unwincing in spray

in this geriatric grove
on the sea-road to Cumana.
To return to the trees,

to decline like this tree,
the burly oak
of Boanerges Ben Jonson!

Or, am I lying
like this felled almond
when I write I look forward to age

a gnarled poet
bearded with the whirlwind,
his metres like thunder?

It is not only the sea,
no, for on windy, green mornings
I read the changes on Morne Coco Mountain,

from flagrant sunrise
to its ashen end;
grey has grown strong to me,

it's no longer neutral,
no longer the dirty flag
of courage going under,

it is speckled with hues
like quartz, it's as
various as boredom,

grey now is a crystal
haze, a dull diamond,
stone-dusted and stoic,

grey is the heart at peace,
tougher than the warrior
as it bestrides factions,

it is the great pause
when the pillars of the temple
rest on Samson's palms

and are held, held,
that moment
when the heavy rock of the world

like a child sleeps
on the trembling shoulders of Atlas
and his own eyes close,

the toil that is balance.
Seneca, that fabled bore,
and his gnarled, laborious Latin

I can read only in fragments
of broken bark, his
heroes tempered by whirlwinds,

who see with the word
senex, with its two eyes,
through the boles of this tree,

beyond joy,
beyond lyrical utterance,
this obdurate almond

going under the sand
with this language, slowly,
by sand grains, by centuries.

The Star-Apple Kingdom

The Schooner *Flight*

---

1   *Adios, Carenage*

In idle August, while the sea soft,
and leaves of brown islands stick to the rim
of this Caribbean, I blow out the light
by the dreamless face of Maria Concepcion
to ship as a seaman on the schooner *Flight*.
Out in the yard turning gray in the dawn,
I stood like a stone and nothing else move
but the cold sea rippling like galvanize
and the nail holes of stars in the sky roof,
till a wind start to interfere with the trees.
I pass me dry neighbor sweeping she yard
as I went downhill, and I nearly said:
"Sweep soft, you witch, 'cause she don't sleep hard,"
but the bitch look through me like I was dead.
A route taxi pull up, park-lights still on.
The driver size up my bags with a grin:
"This time, Shabine, like you really gone!"
I ain't answer the ass, I simply pile in
the back seat and watch the sky burn
above Laventille pink as the gown
in which the woman I left was sleeping,

and I look in the rearview and see a man
exactly like me, and the man was weeping
for the houses, the streets, that whole fucking island.

Christ have mercy on all sleeping things!
From that dog rotting down Wrightson Road
to when I was a dog on these streets;
if loving these islands must be my load,
out of corruption my soul takes wings.
But they had started to poison my soul
with their big house, big car, big-time bohbohl,
coolie, nigger, Syrian, and French Creole,
so I leave it for them and their carnival—
I taking a sea bath, I gone down the road.
I know these islands from Monos to Nassau,
a rusty head sailor with sea-green eyes
that they nickname Shabine, the patois for
any red nigger, and I, Shabine, saw
when these slums of empire was paradise.
I'm just a red nigger who love the sea,
I had a sound colonial education,
I have Dutch, nigger, and English in me,
and either I'm nobody, or I'm a nation,

But Maria Concepcion was all my thought
watching the sea heaving up and down
as the port side of dories, schooners, and yachts
was painted afresh by the strokes of the sun
signing her name with every reflection;
I knew when dark-haired evening put on
her bright silk at sunset, and, folding the sea,
sidled under the sheet with her starry laugh,
that there'd be no rest, there'd be no forgetting.

Is like telling mourners round the graveside
about resurrection, they want the dead back,
so I smile to myself as the bow rope untied
and the *Flight* swing seaward: "Is no use repeating
that the sea have more fish. I ain't want her
dressed in the sexless light of a seraph,
I want those round brown eyes like a marmoset, and
till the day when I can lean back and laugh,
those claws that tickled my back on sweating
Sunday afternoons, like a crab on wet sand."
As I worked, watching the rotting waves come
past the bow that scissor the sea like silk,
I swear to you all, by my mother's milk,
by the stars that shall fly from tonight's furnace,
that I loved them, my children, my wife, my home;
I loved them as poets love the poetry
that kills them, as drowned sailors the sea.

You ever look up from some lonely beach
and see a far schooner? Well, when I write
this poem, each phrase go be soaked in salt;
I go draw and knot every line as tight
as ropes in this rigging; in simple speech
my common language go be the wind,
my pages the sails of the schooner *Flight*.
But let me tell you how this business begin.

Smuggled Scotch for O'Hara, big government man,
between Cedros and the Main, so the Coast Guard couldn't
    touch us,
and the Spanish pirogues always met us halfway,
but a voice kept saying: "Shabine, see this business
of playing pirate?" Well, so said, so done!
That whole racket crash. And I for a woman,
for her laces and silks, Maria Concepcion.
Ay, ay! Next thing I hear, some Commission of Inquiry
was being organized to conduct a big quiz,
with himself as chairman investigating himself.
Well, I knew damn well who the suckers would be,
not that shark in shark skin, but his pilot fish,
khaki-pants red niggers like you and me.
What worse, I fighting with Maria Concepcion,
plates flying and thing, so I swear: "Not again!"
It was mashing up my house and my family.
I was so broke all I needed was shades and a cup
or four shades and four cups in four-cup Port of Spain;
all the silver I had was the coins on the sea.

You saw them ministers in *The Express*,
guardians of the poor—one hand at their back,
and one set o' police only guarding their house,
and the Scotch pouring in through the back door.
As for that minister-monster who smuggled the booze,
that half-Syrian saurian, I got so vex to see
that face thick with powder, the warts, the stone lids
like a dinosaur caked with primordial ooze

by the lightning of flashbulbs sinking in wealth,
that I said: "Shabine, this is shit, understand!"
But he get somebody to kick my crutch out his office
like I was some artist! That bitch was so grand,
couldn't get off his high horse and kick me himself.
I have seen things that would make a slave sick
in this Trinidad, the Limers' Republic.

I couldn't shake the sea noise out of my head,
the shell of my ears sang Maria Concepcion,
so I start salvage diving with a crazy Mick,
name O'Shaugnessy, and a limey named Head;
but this Caribbean so choke with the dead
that when I would melt in emerald water,
whose ceiling rippled like a silk tent,
I saw them corals: brain, fire, sea fans,
dead-men's-fingers, and then, the dead men.
I saw that the powdery sand was their bones
ground white from Senegal to San Salvador,
so, I panic third dive, and surface for a month
in the Seamen's Hostel. Fish broth and sermons.
When I thought of the woe I had brought my wife,
when I saw my worries with that other woman,
I wept under water, salt seeking salt,
for her beauty had fallen on me like a sword
cleaving me from my children, flesh of my flesh!

There was this barge from St. Vincent, but she was too deep
to float her again. When we drank, the limey
got tired of my sobbing for Maria Concepcion.
He said he was getting the bends. Good for him!
The pain in my heart for Maria Concepcion,
the hurt I had done to my wife and children,

was worse than the bends. In the rapturous deep
there was no cleft rock where my soul could hide
like the boobies each sunset, no sandbar of light
where I could rest, like the pelicans know,
so I got raptures once, and I saw God
like a harpooned grouper bleeding, and a far
voice was rumbling, "Shabine, if you leave her,
if you leave her, I shall give you the morning star."
When I left the madhouse I tried other women
but, once they stripped naked, their spiky cunts
bristled like sea eggs and I couldn't dive.
The chaplain came round. I paid him no mind.
Where is my rest place, Jesus? Where is my harbor?
Where is the pillow I will not have to pay for,
and the window I can look from that frames my life?

3   Shabine Leaves the Republic

I had no nation now but the imagination.
After the white man, the niggers didn't want me
when the power swing to their side.
The first chain my hands and apologize, "History";
the next said I wasn't black enough for their pride.
Tell me, what power, on these unknown rocks—
a spray-plane Air Force, the Fire Brigade,
the Red Cross, the Regiment, two, three police dogs
that pass before you finish bawling "Parade!"?
I met History once, but he ain't recognize me,
a parchment Creole, with warts
like an old sea bottle, crawling like a crab

through the holes of shadow cast by the net
of a grille balcony; cream linen, cream hat.
I confront him and shout, "Sir, is Shabine!
They say I'se your grandson. You remember Grandma,
your black cook, at all?" The bitch hawk and spat.
A spit like that worth any number of words.
But that's all them bastards have left us: words.

I no longer believed in the revolution.
I was losing faith in the love of my woman.
I had seen that moment Aleksandr Blok
crystallize in *The Twelve*. Was between
the Police Marine Branch and Hotel Venezuelana
one Sunday at noon. Young men without flags
using shirts, their chests waiting for holes.
They kept marching into the mountains, and
their noise ceased as foam sinks into sand.
They sank in the bright hills like rain, every one
with his own nimbus, leaving shirts in the street,
and the echo of power at the end of the street.
Propeller-blade fans turn over the Senate;
the judges, they say, still sweat in carmine,
on Frederick Street the idlers all marching
by standing still, the Budget turns a new leaf.
In the 12:30 movies the projectors best
not break down, or you go see revolution. Aleksandr Blok
enters and sits in the third row of pit eating choc-
olate cone, waiting for a spaghetti Western with Clint Eastwood and featuring Lee Van Cleef.

4 The Flight, Passing Blanchisseuse

Dusk. The *Flight* passing Blanchisseuse.
Gulls wheel like from a gun again,
and foam gone amber that was white,
lighthouse and star start making friends,
down every beach the long day ends,
and there, on that last stretch of sand,
on a beach bare of all but light,
dark hands start pulling in the seine
of the dark sea, deep, deep inland.

5 Shabine Encounters the Middle Passage

Man, I brisk in the galley first thing next dawn,
brewing li'l coffee; fog coil from the sea
like the kettle steaming when I put it down
slow, slow, 'cause I couldn't believe what I see:
where the horizon was one silver haze,
the fog swirl and swell into sails, so close
that I saw it was sails, my hair grip my skull,
it was horrors, but it was beautiful.
We float through a rustling forest of ships
with sails dry like paper, behind the glass
I saw men with rusty eyeholes like cannons,
and whenever their half-naked crews cross the sun,

right through their tissue, you traced their bones
like leaves against the sunlight; frigates, barkentines,
the backward-moving current swept them on,
and high on their decks I saw great admirals,
Rodney, Nelson, de Grasse, I heard the hoarse orders
they gave those Shabines, and that forest
of masts sail right through the *Flight*,
and all you could hear was the ghostly sound
of waves rustling like grass in a low wind
and the hissing weeds they trailed from the stern;
slowly they heaved past from east to west
like this round world was some cranked water wheel,
every ship pouring like a wooden bucket
dredged from the deep; my memory revolve
on all sailors before me, then the sun
heat the horizon's ring and they was mist.

Next we pass slave ships. Flags of all nations,
our fathers below deck too deep, I suppose,
to hear us shouting. So we stop shouting. Who knows
who his grandfather is, much less his name?
Tomorrow our landfall will be the Barbados.

6   *The Sailor Sings Back to the
    Casuarinas*

You see them on the low hills of Barbados
bracing like windbreaks, needles for hurricanes,
trailing, like masts, the cirrus of torn sails;
when I was green like them, I used to think

those cypresses, leaning against the sea,
that take the sea noise up into their branches,
are not real cypresses but casuarinas.
Now captain just call them Canadian cedars.
But cedars, cypresses, or casuarinas,
whoever called them so had a good cause,
watching their bending bodies wail like women
after a storm, when some schooner came home
with news of one more sailor drowned again.
Once the sound "cypress" used to make more sense
than the green "casuarinas," though, to the wind
whatever grief bent them was all the same,
since they were trees with nothing else in mind
but heavenly leaping or to guard a grave;
but we live like our names and you would have
to be colonial to know the difference,
to know the pain of history words contain,
to love those trees with an inferior love,
and to believe: "Those casuarinas bend
like cypresses, their hair hangs down in rain
like sailors' wives. They're classic trees, and we,
if we live like the names our masters please,
by careful mimicry might become men."

7 *The* Flight *Anchors in*
Castries Harbor

When the stars self were young over Castries,
I loved you alone and I loved the whole world.
What does it matter that our lives are different?

Burdened with the loves of our different children?
When I think of your young face washed by the wind
and your voice that chuckles in the slap of the sea?
The lights are out on La Toc promontory,
except for the hospital. Across at Vigie
the marina arcs keep vigil. I have kept my own
promise, to leave you the one thing I own,
you whom I loved first: my poetry.
We here for one night. Tomorrow, the *Flight* will be gone.

8 *Fight with the Crew*

It had one bitch on board, like he had me mark—
that was the cook, some Vincentian arse
with a skin like a gommier tree, red peeling bark,
and wash-out blue eyes; he wouldn't give me a ease,
like he feel he was white. Had an exercise book,
this same one here, that I was using to write
my poetry, so one day this man snatch it
from my hand, and start throwing it left and right
to the rest of the crew, bawling out, "Catch it,"
and start mincing me like I was some hen
because of the poems. Some case is for fist,
some case is for tholing pin, some is for knife—
this one was for knife. Well, I beg him first,
but he keep reading, "O my children, my wife,"
and playing he crying, to make the crew laugh;
it move like a flying fish, the silver knife
that catch him right in the plump of his calf,
and he faint so slowly, and he turn more white

than he thought he was. I suppose among men
you need that sort of thing. It ain't right
but that's how it is. There wasn't much pain,
just plenty blood, and Vincie and me best friend,
but none of them go fuck with my poetry again.

9   Maria Concepcion & the Book
     of Dreams

The jet that was screeching over the *Flight*
was opening a curtain into the past.
"Dominica ahead!"
                         "It still have Caribs there."
"One day go be planes only, no more boat."
"Vince, God ain't make nigger to fly through the air."
"Progress, Shabine, that's what it's all about.
Progress leaving all we small islands behind."
I was at the wheel, Vince sitting next to me
gaffing. Crisp, bracing day. A high-running sea.
"Progress is something to ask Caribs about.
They kill them by millions, some in war,
some by forced labor dying in the mines
looking for silver, after that niggers; more
progress. Until I see definite signs
that mankind change, Vince, I ain't want to hear.
Progress is history's dirty joke.
Ask that sad green island getting nearer."
Green islands, like mangoes pickled in brine.
In such fierce salt let my wound be healed,
me, in my freshness as a seafarer.

That night, with the sky sparks frosty with fire,
I ran like a Carib through Dominica,
my nose holes choked with memory of smoke;
I heard the screams of my burning children,
I ate the brains of mushrooms, the fungi
of devil's parasols under white, leprous rocks;
my breakfast was leaf mold in leaking forests,
with leaves big as maps, and when I heard noise
of the soldiers' progress through the thick leaves,
though my heart was bursting, I get up and ran
through the blades of balisier sharper than spears;
with the blood of my race, I ran, boy, I ran
with moss-footed speed like a painted bird;
then I fall, but I fall by an icy stream under
cool fountains of fern, and a screaming parrot
catch the dry branches and I drowned at last
in big breakers of smoke; then when that ocean
of black smoke pass, and the sky turn white,
there was nothing but Progress, if Progress is
an iguana as still as a young leaf in sunlight.
I bawl for Maria, and her *Book of Dreams*.

It anchored her sleep, that insomniac's Bible,
a soiled orange booklet with a cyclop's eye
center, from the Dominican Republic.
Its coarse pages were black with the usual
symbols of prophecy, in excited Spanish;
an open palm upright, sectioned and numbered
like a butcher chart, delivered the future.
One night; in a fever, radiantly ill,
she say, "Bring me the book, the end has come."
She said: "I dreamt of whales and a storm,"
but for that dream, the book had no answer.

A next night I dreamed of three old women
featureless as silkworms, stitching my fate,
and I scream at them to come out my house,
and I try beating them away with a broom,
but as they go out, so they crawl back again,
until I start screaming and crying, my flesh
raining with sweat, and she ravage the book
for the dream meaning, and there was nothing;
my nerves melt like a jellyfish—that was when I broke—
they found me round the Savannah, screaming:

All you see me talking to the wind, so you think I mad.
Well, Shabine has bridled the horses of the sea;
you see me watching the sun till my eyeballs seared,
so all you mad people feel Shabine crazy,
but all you ain't know my strength, hear? The coconuts
standing by in their regiments in yellow khaki,
they waiting for Shabine to take over these islands,
and all you best dread the day I am healed
of being a human. All you fate in my hand,
ministers, businessmen, Shabine have you, friend,
I shall scatter your lives like a handful of sand,
I who have no weapon but poetry and
the lances of palms and the sea's shining shield!

10 *Out of the Depths*

Next day, dark sea. A arse-aching dawn.
"Damn wind shift sudden as a woman mind."
The slow swell start cresting like some mountain range

with snow on the top.
                    "Ay, Skipper, sky dark!"
"This ain't right for August."
                    "This light damn strange,
this season, sky should be clear as a field."

A stingray steeplechase across the sea,
tail whipping water, the high man-o'-wars
start reeling inland, quick, quick an archery
of flying fish miss us! Vince say: "You notice?"
and a black-mane squall pounce on the sail
like a dog on a pigeon, and it snap the neck
of the *Flight* and shake it from head to tail.
"Be Jesus, I never see sea get so rough
so fast! That wind come from God back pocket!"
"Where Cap'n headin? Like the man gone blind!"
"If we's to drong, we go drong, Vince, fock-it!"
"Shabine, say your prayers, if life leave you any!"

I have not loved those that I loved enough.
Worse than the mule kick of Kick-'Em-Jenny
Channel, rain start to pelt the *Flight* between
mountains of water. If I was frighten?
The tent poles of water spouts bracing the sky
start wobbling, clouds unstitch at the seams
and sky water drench us, and I hear myself cry,
"I'm the drowned sailor in her *Book of Dreams*."
I remembered them ghost ships, I saw me corkscrewing
to the sea bed of sea worms, fathom pass fathom,
my jaw clench like a fist, and only one thing
hold me, trembling, how my family safe home.
Then a strength like it seize me and the strength said:

"I from backward people who still fear God."
Let Him, in His might, heave Leviathan upward
by the winch of His will, the beast pouring lace
from his sea-bottom bed; and that was the faith
that had fade from a child in the Methodist chapel
in Chisel Street, Castries, when the whale-bell
sang service and, in hard pews ribbed like the whale,
proud with despair, we sang how our race
survive the sea's maw, our history, our peril,
and now I was ready for whatever death will.
But if that storm had strength, was in Cap'n face,
beard beading with spray, tears salting his eyes,
crucify to his post, that nigger hold fast
to that wheel, man, like the cross held Jesus,
and the wounds of his eyes like they crying for us,
and I feeding him white rum, while every crest
with Leviathan-lash make the *Flight* quail
like two criminal. Whole night, with no rest,
till red-eyed like dawn, we watch our travail
subsiding, subside, and there was no more storm.
And the noon sea get calm as Thy Kingdom come.

11   *After the Storm*

There's a fresh light that follows a storm
while the whole sea still havoc; in its bright wake
I saw the veiled face of Maria Concepcion
marrying the ocean, then drifting away
in the widening lace of her bridal train

with white gulls her bridesmaids, till she was gone.
I wanted nothing after that day.
Across my own face, like the face of the sun,
a light rain was falling, with the sea calm.

Fall gently, rain, on the sea's upturned face
like a girl showering; make these islands fresh
as Shabine once knew them! Let every trace,
every hot road, smell like clothes she just press
and sprinkle with drizzle. I finish dream;
whatever the rain wash and the sun iron:
the white clouds, the sea and sky with one seam,
is clothes enough for my nakedness.
Though my *Flight* never pass the incoming tide
of this inland sea beyond the loud reefs
of the final Bahamas, I am satisfied
if my hand gave voice to one people's grief.
Open the map. More islands there, man,
than peas on a tin plate, all different size,
one thousand in the Bahamas alone,
from mountains to low scrub with coral keys,
and from this bowsprit, I bless every town,
the blue smell of smoke in hills behind them,
and the one small road winding down them like twine
to the roofs below; I have only one theme:

The bowsprit, the arrow, the longing, the lunging heart—
the flight to a target whose aim we'll never know,
vain search for one island that heals with its harbor
and a guiltless horizon, where the almond's shadow
doesn't injure the sand. There are so many islands!
As many islands as the stars at night
on that branched tree from which meteors are shaken

like falling fruit around the schooner *Flight*.
But things must fall, and so it always was,
on one hand Venus, on the other Mars;
fall, and are one, just as this earth is one
island in archipelagoes of stars.
My first friend was the sea. Now, is my last.
I stop talking now. I work, then I read,
cotching under a lantern hooked to the mast.
I try to forget what happiness was,
and when that don't work, I study the stars.
Sometimes is just me, and the soft-scissored foam
as the deck turn white and the moon open
a cloud like a door, and the light over me
is a road in white moonlight taking me home.
Shabine sang to you from the depths of the sea.

In the Virgins

FOR BILL AND PAT STRACHAN

You can't put in the ground swell of the organ
from the Christiansted, St. Croix, Anglican Church
behind the paratrooper's voice: "Turned cop
after Vietnam. I made thirty jumps."
Bells punish the dead street and pigeons lurch
from the stone belfry, opening their chutes,
circling until the rings of ringing stop.
"Salud!" The paratrooper's glass is raised.
The congregation rises to its feet
like a patrol, with scuffling shoes and boots,
repeating orders as the organ thumps:
"Praise Ye the Lord. The Lord's name be praised."

You cannot hear, beyond the quiet harbor,
the breakers cannonading on the bruised
horizon, or the charter engines gunning for
Buck Island. The only war here is a war
of silence between blue sky and sea,
and just one voice, the marching choir's, is raised
to draft new conscripts with the ancient cry
of "Onward, Christian Soldiers," into pews
half-empty still, or like a glass, half-full.
Pinning itself to a cornice, a gull
hangs like a medal from the serge-blue sky.

Are these boats all? Is the blue water all?
The rocks surpliced with lace where they are moored,
dinghy, catamaran, and racing yawl,
nodding to the ground swell of "Praise the Lord"?
Wesley and Watts, their evangelical light
lanced down the mine shafts to our chapel pew,
its beam gritted with motes of anthracite
that drifted on us in our chapel benches:
from God's slow-grinding mills in Lancashire,
ash on the dead mired in Flanders' trenches,
as a gray drizzle now defiles the view

of this blue harbor, framed in windows where
two yellow palm fronds, jerked by the wind's rein,
agree like horses' necks, and nodding bear,
slow as a hearse, a haze of tasseled rain,
and, as the weather changes in a child,
the paradisal day outside grows dark,
the yachts flutter like moths in a gray jar,
the martial voices fade in thunder, while
across the harbor, like a timid lure,
a rainbow casts its seven-colored arc.

Tonight, now Sunday has been put to rest.
Altar lights ride the black glass where the yachts
stiffly repeat themselves and phosphoresce
with every ripple—the wide parking lots
of tidal affluence—and every mast
sways the night's dial as its needle veers
to find the station which is truly peace.
Like neon lasers shot across the bars
discos blast out the music of the spheres,
and, one by one, science infects the stars.

Sabbaths, W.I.

Those villages stricken with the melancholia of Sunday,
in all of whose ocher streets one dog is sleeping

those volcanoes like ashen roses, or the incurable sore
of poverty, around whose puckered mouth thin boys are
selling yellow sulphur stone

the burnt banana leaves that used to dance
the river whose bed is made of broken bottles
the cocoa grove where a bird whose cry sounds green and
yellow and in the lights under the leaves crested with
orange flame has forgotten its flute

gommiers peeling from sunburn still wrestling to escape the sea

the dead lizard turning blue as stone

those rivers, threads of spittle, that forgot the old music

that dry, brief esplanade under the drier sea almonds
where the dry old men sat

watching a white schooner stuck in the branches

and playing draughts with the moving frigate birds

those hillsides like broken pots
those ferns that stamped their skeletons on the skin

and those roads that begin reciting their names at vespers

mention them and they will stop
those crabs that were willing to let an epoch pass
those herons like spinsters that doubted their reflections
inquiring, inquiring

those nettles that waited
those Sundays, those Sundays

those Sundays when the lights at the road's end were an occasion

those Sundays when my mother lay on her back
those Sundays when the sisters gathered like white moths
round their street lantern

and cities passed us by on the horizon

The Sea Is History

Where are your monuments, your battles, martyrs?
Where is your tribal memory? Sirs,
in that gray vault. The sea. The sea
has locked them up. The sea is History.

First, there was the heaving oil,
heavy as chaos;
then, like a light at the end of a tunnel,

the lantern of a caravel,
and that was Genesis.
Then there were the packed cries,
the shit, the moaning:

Exodus.
Bone soldered by coral to bone,
mosaics
mantled by the benediction of the shark's shadow,

that was the Ark of the Covenant.
Then came from the plucked wires
of sunlight on the sea floor

the plangent harps of the Babylonian bondage,
as the white cowries clustered like manacles
on the drowned women,

and those were the ivory bracelets
of the Song of Solomon,
but the ocean kept turning blank pages

looking for History.
Then came the men with eyes heavy as anchors
who sank without tombs,

brigands who barbecued cattle,
leaving their charred ribs like palm leaves on the shore,
then the foaming, rabid maw

of the tidal wave swallowing Port Royal,
and that was Jonah,
but where is your Renaissance?

Sir, it is locked in them sea sands
out there past the reef's moiling shelf,
where the men-o'-war floated down;

strop on these goggles, I'll guide you there myself.
It's all subtle and submarine,
through colonnades of coral,

past the gothic windows of sea fans
to where the crusty grouper, onyx-eyed,
blinks, weighted by its jewels, like a bald queen;

and these groined caves with barnacles
pitted like stone
are our cathedrals,

and the furnace before the hurricanes:
Gomorrah. Bones ground by windmills
into marl and cornmeal,

and that was Lamentations—
that was just Lamentations,
it was not History;

then came, like scum on the river's drying lip,
the brown reeds of villages
mantling and congealing into towns,

and at evening, the midges' choirs,
and above them, the spires
lancing the side of God

as His son set, and that was the New Testament.

Then came the white sisters clapping
to the waves' progress,
and that was Emancipation—

jubilation, O jubilation—
vanishing swiftly
as the sea's lace dries in the sun,

but that was not History,
that was only faith,
and then each rock broke into its own nation;

then came the synod of flies,
then came the secretarial heron,
then came the bullfrog bellowing for a vote,

fireflies with bright ideas
and bats like jetting ambassadors
and the mantis, like khaki police,

and the furred caterpillars of judges
examining each case closely,
and then in the dark ears of ferns

and in the salt chuckle of rocks
with their sea pools, there was the sound
like a rumor without any echo

of History, really beginning.

Egypt, Tobago

FOR N.M.

There is a shattered palm
on this fierce shore,
its plumes the rusting helmet of a dead warrior.

Numb Antony, in the torpor
stretching her inert
sex near him like a sleeping cat,
knows his heart is the real desert.

Over the dunes
of her heaving,
to his heart's drumming
fades the mirage of the legions,

across love-tousled sheets,
the triremes fading.
At the carved door of her temple
a fly wrings its message.

He brushes a damp hair
away from an ear
as perfect as a sleeping child's.
He stares, inert, the fallen column.

He lies like a copper palm
tree at three in the afternoon
by a hot sea
and a river, in Egypt, Tobago.

Her salt marsh dries in the heat
where he foundered
without armor.
He exchanged an empire for her beads of sweat,

the uproar of arenas,
the changing surf
of senators, for
this silent ceiling over silent sand—

this grizzled bear, whose fur,
moulting, is silvered—
for this quick fox with her
sweet stench. By sleep dismembered,

his head
is in Egypt, his feet
in Rome, his groin a desert
trench with its dead soldier.

He drifts a finger
through her stiff hair
crisp as a mare's fountaining tail.
Shadows creep up the palace tile.

He is too tired to move;
a groan would waken
trumpets, one more gesture,
war. His glare,

a shield
reflecting fires,
a brass brow that cannot frown
at carnage, sweats the sun's force.

It is not the turmoil
of autumnal lust,
its treacheries, that drove
him, fired and grimed with dust,

this far, not even love,
but a great rage without
clamor, that grew great
because its depth is quiet;

it hears the river
of her young brown blood,
it feels the whole sky quiver
with her blue eyelid.

She sleeps with the soft engine of a child,

that sleep which scythes
the stalks of lances, fells the
harvest of legions
with nothing for its knives,
that makes Caesars,

sputtering at flies,
slapping their foreheads
with the laurel's imprint,
drunkards, comedians.

All-humbling sleep, whose peace
is sweet as death,
whose silence has
all the sea's weight and volubility,

who swings this globe by a hair's trembling breath.

Shattered and wild and
palm-crowned Antony,
rusting in Egypt,
ready to lose the world,
to Actium and sand,

everything else
is vanity, but this tenderness
for a woman not his mistress
but his sleeping child.

The sky is cloudless. The afternoon is mild.

The Saddhu of Couva

FOR KENNETH RAMCHAND

When sunset, a brass gong,
vibrate through Couva,
is then I see my soul, swiftly unsheathed,
like a white cattle bird growing more small
over the ocean of the evening canes,
and I sit quiet, waiting for it to return
like a hog-cattle blistered with mud,
because, for my spirit, India is too far.
And to that gong
sometimes bald clouds in saffron robes assemble
sacred to the evening,
sacred even to Ramlochan,
singing Indian hits from his jute hammock
while evening strokes the flanks
and silver horns of his maroon taxi,
as the mosquitoes whine their evening mantras,
my friend Anopheles, on the sitar,
and the fireflies making every dusk Divali.

I knot my head with a cloud,
my white mustache bristle like horns,
my hands are brittle as the pages of Ramayana.
Once the sacred monkeys multiplied like branches
in the ancient temples; I did not miss them,

because these fields sang of Bengal,
behind Ramlochan Repairs there was Uttar Pradesh;
but time roars in my ears like a river,
old age is a conflagration
as fierce as the cane fires of crop time.
I will pass through these people like a cloud,
they will see a white bird beating the evening sea
of the canes behind Couva,
and who will point it as my soul unsheathed?
Neither the bridegroom in beads,
nor the bride in her veils,
their sacred language on the cinema hoardings.

I talked too damn much on the Couva Village Council.
I talked too softly, I was always drowned
by the loudspeakers in front of the stores
or the loudspeakers with the greatest pictures.
I am best suited to stalk like a white cattle bird
on legs like sticks, with sticking to the Path
between the canes on a district road at dusk.
Playing the Elder. There are no more elders.
Is only old people.

My friends spit on the government.
I do not think is just the government.
Suppose all the gods too old,
Suppose they dead and they burning them,
supposing when some cane cutter
start chopping up snakes with a cutlass
he is severing the snake-armed god,
and suppose some hunter has caught
Hanuman in his mischief in a monkey cage.
Suppose all the gods were killed by electric light?

Sunset, a bonfire, roars in my ears;
embers of blown swallows dart and cry,
like women distracted,
around its cremation.
I ascend to my bed of sweet sandalwood.

R.T.S.L.

(1917–1977)

As for that other thing
which comes when the eyelid is glazed
and the wax gleam
from the unwrinkled forehead
asks no more questions
of the dry mouth,

whether they open the heart like a shirt
to release a rage of swallows,
whether the brain
is a library for worms,
on the instant of that knowledge
of the moment
when everything became so stiff,

so formal with ironical adieux,
organ and choir,
and I must borrow a black tie,
and at what moment in the oration
shall I break down and weep—

there was the startle of wings
breaking from the closing cage
of your body, your fist unclenching
these pigeons circling serenely
over the page,

and,
as the parentheses lock like a gate
1917 to 1977,
the semicircles close to form a face,
a world, a wholeness,
an unbreakable O,
and something that once had a fearful name
walks from the thing that used to wear its name,
transparent, exact representative,
so that we can see through it
churches, cars, sunlight,
and the Boston Common,
not needing any book.

Forest of Europe

FOR JOSEPH BRODSKY

The last leaves fell like notes from a piano
and left their ovals echoing in the ear;
with gawky music stands, the winter forest
looks like an empty orchestra, its lines
ruled on these scattered manuscripts of snow.

The inlaid copper laurel of an oak
shines through the brown-bricked glass above your head
as bright as whiskey, while the wintry breath
of lines from Mandelstam, which you recite,
uncoils as visibly as cigarette smoke.

"The rustling of ruble notes by the lemon Neva."
Under your exile's tongue, crisp under heel,
the gutturals crackle like decaying leaves,
the phrase from Mandelstam circles with light
in a brown room, in barren Oklahoma.

There is a Gulag Archipelago
under this ice, where the salt, mineral spring
of the long Trail of Tears runnels these plains
as hard and open as a herdsman's face
sun-cracked and stubbled with unshaven snow.

Growing in whispers from the Writers' Congress,
the snow circles like cossacks round the corpse
of a tired Choctaw till it is a blizzard
of treaties and white papers as we lose
sight of the single human through the cause.

So every spring these branches load their shelves,
like libraries with newly published leaves,
till waste recycles them—paper to snow—
but, at zero of suffering, one mind
lasts like this oak with a few brazen leaves.

As the train passed the forest's tortured icons,
the floes clanging like freight yards, then the spires
of frozen tears, the stations screeching steam,
he drew them in a single winter's breath
whose freezing consonants turned into stones.

He saw the poetry in forlorn stations
under clouds vast as Asia, through districts
that could gulp Oklahoma like a grape,
not these tree-shaded prairie halts but space
so desolate it mocked destinations.

Who is that dark child on the parapets
of Europe, watching the evening river mint
its sovereigns stamped with power, not with poets,
the Thames and the Neva rustling like banknotes,
then, black on gold, the Hudson's silhouettes?

From frozen Neva to the Hudson pours,
under the airport domes, the echoing stations,

the tributary of emigrants whom exile
has made as classless as the common cold,
citizens of a language that is now yours,

and every February, every "last autumn,"
you write far from the threshing harvesters
folding wheat like a girl plaiting her hair,
far from Russia's canals quivering with sunstroke,
a man living with English in one room.

The tourist archipelagoes of my South
are prisons too, corruptible, and though
there is no harder prison than writing verse,
what's poetry, if it is worth its salt,
but a phrase men can pass from hand to mouth?

From hand to mouth, across the centuries,
the bread that lasts when systems have decayed,
when, in his forest of barbed-wire branches,
a prisoner circles, chewing the one phrase
whose music will last longer than the leaves,

whose condensation is the marble sweat
of angels' foreheads, which will never dry
till Borealis shuts the peacock lights
of its slow fan from L.A. to Archangel,
and memory needs nothing to repeat.

Frightened and starved, with divine fever
Osip Mandelstam shook, and every
metaphor shuddered him with ague,
each vowel heavier than a boundary stone,
"to the rustling of ruble notes by the lemon Neva,"

but now that fever is a fire whose glow
warms our hands, Joseph, as we grunt like primates
exchanging gutturals in this winter cave
of a brown cottage, while in drifts outside
mastodons force their systems through the snow.

Koenig of the River

Koenig knew now there was no one on the river.
Entering its brown mouth choking with lilies
and curtained with midges, Koenig poled the shallop
past the abandoned ferry and the ferry piles
coated with coal dust. Staying aboard, he saw, up
in a thick meadow, a sand-colored mule,
untethered, with no harness, and no signs
of habitation round the ruined factory wheel
locked hard in rust, and through whose spokes the vines
of wild yam leaves leant from overweight;
the wild bananas in the yellowish sunlight
were dugged like aching cows with unmilked fruit.
This was the last of the productive mines.
Only the vegetation here looked right.
A crab of pain scuttled shooting up his foot
and fastened on his neck, at the brain's root.
He felt his reason curling back like parchment
in this fierce torpor. Well, he no longer taxed
and tired what was left of his memory;
he should thank heaven he had escaped the sea,
and anyway, he had demanded to be sent
here with the others—why get this river vexed
with his complaints? Koenig wanted to sing,
suddenly, if only to keep the river company—
this was a river, and Koenig, his name meant King.

They had all caught the missionary fever:
they were prepared to expiate the sins
of savages, to tame them as he would tame this river
subtly, as it flowed, accepting its bends;
he had seen how other missionaries met their ends—
swinging in the wind, like a dead clapper when
a bell is broken, if that sky was a bell—
for treating savages as if they were men,
and frightening them with talk of Heaven and Hell.
But I have forgotten our journey's origins,
mused Koenig, and our purpose. He knew it was noble,
based on some phrase, forgotten, from the Bible,
but he felt bodiless, like a man stumbling from
the pages of a novel, not a forest,
written a hundred years ago. He stroked his uniform,
clogged with the hooked burrs that had tried
to pull him, like the other drowning hands whom
his panic abandoned. The others had died,
like real men, by death. I, Koenig, am a ghost,
ghost-king of rivers. Well, even ghosts must rest.
If he knew he was lost he was not lost.
It was when you pretended that you were a fool.
He banked and leaned tiredly on the pole.
If I'm a character called Koenig, then I
shall dominate my future like a fiction
in which there is a real river and real sky,
so I'm not really tired, and should push on.

The lights between the leaves were beautiful,
and, as in that far life, now he was grateful
for any pool of light between the dull, usual
clouds of life: a sunspot haloed his tonsure;
silver and copper coins danced on the river;

his head felt warm—the light danced on his skull
like a benediction. Koenig closed his eyes,
and he felt blessed. It made direction sure.
He leant on the pole. He must push on some more.
He said his name. His voice sounded German,
then he said "river," but what was German
if he alone could hear it? *Ich spreche Deutsch*
sounded as genuine as his name in English,
Koenig in Deutsch, and, in English, King.
Did the river want to be called anything?
He asked the river. The river said nothing.

Around the bend the river poured its silver
like some remorseful mine, giving and giving
everything green and white: white sky, white
water, and the dull green like a drumbeat
of the slow-sliding forest, the green heat;
then, on some sandbar, a mirage ahead:
fabric of muslin sails, spiderweb rigging,
a schooner, foundered on black river mud,
was rising slowly up from the riverbed,
and a top-hatted native reading an inverted
newspaper.
                    "Where's our Queen?" Koenig shouted.
"Where's our Kaiser?"
                    The nigger disappeared.
Koenig felt that he himself was being read
like the newspaper or a hundred-year-old novel.
"The Queen dead! Kaiser dead!" the voices shouted.
And it flashed through him those trunks were not wood
but that the ghosts of slaughtered Indians stood
there in the mangroves, their eyes like fireflies

in the green dark, and that like hummingbirds
they sailed rather than ran between the trees.
The river carried him past his shouted words.
The schooner had gone down without a trace.
"There was a time when we ruled everything,"
Koenig sang to his corrugated white reflection.
"The German Eagle and the British Lion,
we ruled worlds wider than this river flows,
worlds with dyed elephants, with tassled howdahs,
tigers that carried the striped shade when they rose
from their palm coverts; men shall not see these days
again; our flags sank with the sunset on the dhows
of Egypt; we ruled rivers as huge as the Nile,
the Ganges, and the Congo, we tamed, we ruled
you when our empires reached their blazing peak."
This was a small creek somewhere in the world,
never mind where—victory was in sight.
Koenig laughed and spat in the brown creek.
The mosquitoes now were singing to the night
that rose up from the river, the fog uncurled
under the mangroves. Koenig clenched each fist
around his barge-pole scepter, as a mist
rises from the river and the page goes white.

The Star-Apple Kingdom

There were still shards of an ancient pastoral
in those shires of the island where the cattle drank
their pools of shadow from an older sky,
surviving from when the landscape copied such subjects as
"Herefords at Sunset in the Valley of the Wye."
The mountain water that fell white from the mill wheel
sprinkling like petals from the star-apple trees,
and all of the windmills and sugar mills moved by mules
on the treadmill of Monday to Monday, would repeat
in tongues of water and wind and fire, in tongues
of Mission School pickaninnies, like rivers remembering
their source, Parish Trelawny, Parish St. David, Parish
St. Andrew, the names afflicting the pastures,
the lime groves and fences of marl stone and the cattle
with a docile longing, an epochal content.
And there were, like old wedding lace in an attic,
among the boas and parasols and the tea-colored
daguerreotypes, hints of an epochal happiness
as ordered and infinite to the child
as the great house road to the Great House
down a perspective of casuarinas plunging green manes
in time to the horses, an orderly life
reduced by lorgnettes day and night, one disc the sun,
the other the moon, reduced into a pier glass:

nannies diminished to dolls, mahogany stairways
no larger than those of an album in which
the flash of cutlery yellows, as gamboge as
the piled cakes of teatime on that latticed
bougainvillaea verandah that looked down toward
a prospect of Cuyp-like Herefords under a sky
lurid as a porcelain souvenir with these words:
"Herefords at Sunset in the Valley of the Wye."

Strange, that the rancor of hatred hid in that dream
of slow rivers and lily-like parasols, in snaps
of fine old colonial families, curled at the edge
not from age or from fire or the chemicals, no, not at all,
but because, off at its edges, innocently excluded
stood the groom, the cattle boy, the housemaid, the gardeners,
the tenants, the good Negroes down in the village,
their mouths in the locked jaw of a silent scream.
A scream which would open the doors to swing wildly
all night, that was bringing in heavier clouds,
more black smoke than cloud, frightening the cattle
in whose bulging eyes the Great House diminished;
a scorching wind of a scream
that began to extinguish the fireflies,
that dried the water mill creaking to a stop
as it was about to pronounce Parish Trelawny
all over, in the ancient pastoral voice,
a wind that blew all without bending anything,
neither the leaves of the album nor the lime groves;
blew Nanny floating back in white from a feather
to a chimerical, chemical pin speck that shrank
the drinking Herefords to brown porcelain cows
on a mantelpiece, Trelawny trembling with dusk,
the scorched pastures of the old benign Custos; blew

far the decent servants and the lifelong cook,
and shriveled to a shard that ancient pastoral
of dusk in a gilt-edged frame now catching the evening sun
in Jamaica, making both epochs one.

He looked out from the Great House windows on
clouds that still held the fragrance of fire,
he saw the Botanical Gardens officially drown
in a formal dusk, where governors had strolled
and black gardeners had smiled over glinting shears
at the lilies of parasols on the floating lawns,
the flame trees obeyed his will and lowered their wicks,
the flowers tightened their fists in the name of thrift,
the porcelain lamps of ripe cocoa, the magnolia's jet
dimmed on the one circuit with the ginger lilies
and left a lonely bulb on the verandah,
and, had his mandate extended to that ceiling
of star-apple candelabra, he would have ordered
the sky to sleep, saying, I'm tired,
save the starlight for victories, we can't afford it,
leave the moon on for one more hour, and that's it.
But though his power, the given mandate, extended
from tangerine daybreaks to star-apple dusks,
his hand could not dam that ceaseless torrent of dust
that carried the shacks of the poor, to their root-rock music,
down the gullies of Yallahs and August Town,
to lodge them on thorns of maca, with their rags
crucified by cactus, tins, old tires, cartons;
from the black Warieka Hills the sky glowed fierce as
the dials of a million radios,
a throbbing sunset that glowed like a grid
where the dread beat rose from the jukebox of Kingston.

He saw the fountains dried of quadrilles, the water-music
of the country dancers, the fiddlers like fifes
put aside. He had to heal
this malarial island in its bath of bay leaves,
its forests tossing with fever, the dry cattle
groaning like winches, the grass that kept shaking
its head to remember its name. No vowels left
in the mill wheel, the river. Rock stone. Rock stone.

The mountains rolled like whales through phosphorous stars,
as he swayed like a stone down fathoms into sleep,
drawn by that magnet which pulls down half the world
between a star and a star, by that black power
that has the assassin dreaming of snow,
that poleaxes the tyrant to a sleeping child.
The house is rocking at anchor, but as he falls
his mind is a mill wheel in moonlight,
and he hears, in the sleep of his moonlight, the drowned
bell of Port Royal's cathedral, sees the copper pennies
of bubbles rising from the empty eye-pockets
of green buccaneers, the parrot fish floating
from the frayed shoulders of pirates, sea horses
drawing gowned ladies in their liquid promenade
across the moss-green meadows of the sea;
he heard the drowned choirs under Palisadoes,
a hymn ascending to earth from a heaven inverted
by water, a crab climbing the steeple,
and he climbed from that submarine kingdom
as the evening lights came on in the institute,
the scholars lamplit in their own aquarium,
he saw them mouthing like parrot fish, as he passed
upward from that baptism, their history lessons,

the bubbles like ideas which he could not break:
Jamaica was captured by Penn and Venables,
Port Royal perished in a cataclysmic earthquake.

Before the coruscating façades of cathedrals
from Santiago to Caracas, where penitential archbishops
washed the feet of paupers (a parenthetical moment
that made the Caribbean a baptismal font,
turned butterflies to stone, and whitened like doves
the buzzards circling municipal garbage),
the Caribbean was borne like an elliptical basin
in the hands of acolytes, and a people were absolved
of a history which they did not commit;
the slave pardoned his whip, and the dispossessed
said the rosary of islands for three hundred years,
a hymn that resounded like the hum of the sea
inside a sea cave, as their knees turned to stone,
while the bodies of patriots were melting down walls
still crusted with mute outcries of La Revolución!
"San Salvador, pray for us, St. Thomas, San Domingo,
ora pro nobis, intercede for us, Sancta Lucia
of no eyes," and when the circular chaplet
reached the last black bead of Sancta Trinidad
they began again, their knees drilled into stone,
where Colón had begun, with San Salvador's bead,
beads of black colonies round the necks of Indians.
And while they prayed for an economic miracle,
ulcers formed on the municipal portraits,
the hotels went up, and the casinos and brothels,
and the empires of tobacco, sugar, and bananas,
until a black woman, shawled like a buzzard,
climbed up the stairs and knocked at the door
of his dream, whispering in the ear of the keyhole:

"Let me in, I'm finished with praying, I'm the Revolution.
I am the darker, the older America."

She was as beautiful as a stone in the sunrise,
her voice had the gutturals of machine guns
across khaki deserts where the cactus flower
detonates like grenades, her sex was the slit throat
of an Indian, her hair had the blue-black sheen of the crow.
She was a black umbrella blown inside out
by the wind of revolution, La Madre Dolorosa,
a black rose of sorrow, a black mine of silence,
raped wife, empty mother, Aztec virgin
transfixed by arrows from a thousand guitars,
a stone full of silence, which, if it gave tongue
to the tortures done in the name of the Father,
would curdle the blood of the marauding wolf,
the fountain of generals, poets, and cripples
who danced without moving over their graves
with each revolution; her Caesarean was stitched
by the teeth of machine guns, and every sunset
she carried the Caribbean's elliptical basin
as she had once carried the penitential napkins
to be the footbath of dictators, Trujillo, Machado,
and those whose faces had yellowed like posters
on municipal walls. Now she stroked his hair
until it turned white, but she would not understand
that he wanted no other power but peace,
that he wanted a revolution without any bloodshed,
he wanted a history without any memory,
streets without statues,
and a geography without myth. He wanted no armies
but those regiments of bananas, thick lances of cane,
and he sobbed, "I am powerless, except for love."

She faded from him, because he could not kill;
she shrank to a bat that hung day and night
in the back of his brain. He rose in his dream.

The soul, which was his body made as thin
as its reflection and invulnerable
without its clock, was losing track of time;
it walked the mountain tracks of the Maroons,
it swung with Gordon from the creaking gibbet,
it bought a pack of peppermints and cashews
from one of the bandanna'd mammies outside the ward,
it heard his breath pitched to the decibels
of the peanut vendors' carts, it entered a municipal wall
stirring the slogans that shrieked his name: SAVIOR!
and others: LACKEY! he melted like a spoon
through the alphabet soup of CIA, PNP, OPEC,
that resettled once he passed through with this thought:
I should have foreseen those seraphs with barbed-wire hair,
beards like burst mattresses, and wild eyes of garnet,
who nestled the Coptic Bible to their ribs, would
call me Joshua, expecting him to bring down Babylon
by Wednesday, after the fall of Jericho; yes, yes,
I should have seen the cunning bitterness of the rich
who left me no money but these mandates:

His aerial mandate, which
contained the crows whose circuit
was this wedding band that married him to his island.
His marine mandate, which
was the fishing limits
which the shark scissored like silk with its teeth
between Key West and Havana;

his terrestrial:
the bled hills rusted with bauxite;
paradisal:
the chimneys like angels sheathed in aluminum.

In shape like a cloud
he saw the face of his father,
the hair like white cirrus blown back
in a photographic wind,
the mouth of mahogany winced shut,
the eyes lidded, resigned
to the first compromise,
the last ultimatum,
the first and last referendum.

One morning the Caribbean was cut up
by seven prime ministers who bought the sea in bolts—
one thousand miles of aquamarine with lace trimmings,
one million yards of lime-colored silk,
one mile of violet, leagues of cerulean satin—
who sold it at a markup to the conglomerates,
the same conglomerates who had rented the water spouts
for ninety-nine years in exchange for fifty ships,
who retailed it in turn to the ministers
with only one bank account, who then resold it
in ads for the Caribbean Economic Community,
till everyone owned a little piece of the sea,
from which some made saris, some made bandannas;
the rest was offered on trays to white cruise ships
taller than the post office; then the dogfights
began in the cabinets as to who had first sold
the archipelago for this chain store of islands.

Now a tree of grenades was his star-apple kingdom,
over fallow pastures his crows patrolled,
he felt his fist involuntarily tighten
into a talon that was strangling five doves,
the mountains loomed leaden under martial law,
the suburban gardens flowered with white paranoia
next to the bougainvillaeas of astonishing April;
the rumors were a rain that would not fall:
that enemy intelligence had alerted the roaches'
quivering antennae, that bats flew like couriers,
transmitting secrets between the embassies;
over dials in the war rooms, the agents waited
for a rifle crack from Havana; down shuttered avenues
roared a phalanx of Yamahas. They left
a hole in the sky that closed on silence.

He didn't hear the roar of the motorcycles
diminish in circles like those of the water mill
in a far childhood; he was drowned in sleep;
he slept, without dreaming, the sleep after love
in the mineral oblivion of night
whose flesh smells of cocoa, whose teeth are white
as coconut meat, whose breath smells of ginger,
whose braids are scented like sweet-potato vines
in furrows still pungent with the sun.
He slept the sleep that wipes out history,
he slept like the islands on the breast of the sea,
like a child again in her star-apple kingdom.

Tomorrow the sea would gleam like nails
under a zinc sky where the barren frangipani
was hammered, a horizon without liners;

tomorrow the heavy caravels of clouds would wreck
and dissolve in their own foam on the reefs
of the mountains, tomorrow a donkey's yawn
would saw the sky in half, and at dawn
would come the noise of a government groaning uphill.
But now she held him, as she holds us all,
her history-orphaned islands, she to whom
we came late as our muse, our mother,
who suckled the islands, who, when she grows old
with her breasts wrinkled like eggplants
is the head-tie mother, the bleached-sheets-on-the-river-rocks
        mother,
the gospel mother, the t'ank-you-parson mother
who turns into mahogany, the lignum-vitae mother,
her sons like thorns,
her daughters dry gullies that give birth to stones,
who was, in our childhood, the housemaid and the cook,
the young grand' who polished the plaster figure
of Clio, muse of history, in her seashell grotto
in the Great House parlor, Anadyomene washed
in the deep Atlantic heave of her housemaid's hymn.

In the indigo dawn the palms unclenched their fists,
his eyes opened the flowers, and he lay as still
as the waterless mill wheel. The sun's fuse caught,
it hissed on the edge of the skyline, and day exploded
its remorseless avalanche of dray carts and curses,
the roaring oven of Kingston, its sky as fierce
as the tin box of a patties cart. Down the docks
between the Levantine smells of the warehouses
nosed the sea wind with its odor of a dog's damp fur.
He lathered in anger and refreshed his love.

He was lathered like a horse, but the instant
the shower crowned him and he closed his eyes,
he was a bride under lace, remarrying his country,
a child drawn by the roars of the mill wheel's electorate,
those vows reaffirmed; he dressed, went down to breakfast,
and sitting again at the mahogany surface
of the breakfast table, its dark hide as polished
as the sheen of mares, saw his father's face
and his own face blent there, and looked out
to the drying garden and its seeping pond.

What was the Caribbean? A green pond mantling
behind the Great House columns of Whitehall,
behind the Greek façades of Washington,
with bloated frogs squatting on lily pads
like islands, islands that coupled as sadly as turtles
engendering islets, as the turtle of Cuba
mounting Jamaica engendered the Caymans, as, behind
the hammerhead turtle of Haiti-San Domingo
trailed the little turtles from Tortuga to Tobago;
he followed the bobbing trek of the turtles
leaving America for the open Atlantic,
felt his own flesh loaded like the pregnant beaches
with their moon-guarded eggs—they yearned for Africa,
they were lemmings drawn by magnetic memory
to an older death, to broader beaches
where the coughing of lions was dumbed by breakers.
Yes, he could understand their natural direction
but they would drown, sea eagles circling them,
and the languor of frigates that do not beat wings,
and he closed his eyes, and felt his jaw drop
again with the weight of that silent scream.

He cried out at the turtles as one screams at children
with the anger of love, it was the same scream
which, in his childhood, had reversed an epoch
that had bent back the leaves of his star-apple kingdom,
made streams race uphill, pulled the water wheel backwards
like the wheels in a film, and at that outcry,
from the raw ropes and tendons of his throat,
the sea buzzards receded and receded into specks,
and the osprey vanished.
                              On the knee-hollowed steps
of the crusted cathedral, there was a woman in black,
the black of moonless nights, within whose eyes
shone seas in starlight like the glint of knives
(the one who had whispered to the keyhole of his ear),
washing the steps, and she heard it first.
She was one of a flowing black river of women
who bore elliptical basins to the feet of paupers
on the Day of Thorns, who bore milk pails to cows
in a pastoral sunrise, who bore baskets on their heads
down the haemophilic red hills of Haiti,
now with the squeezed rag dripping from her hard hands
the way that vinegar once dropped from a sponge,
but she heard as a dog hears, as all the underdogs
of the world hear, the pitched shriek of silence.
Star-apples rained to the ground in that silence,
the silence was the green of cities undersea,
and the silence lasted for half an hour
in that single second, a seashell silence, resounding
with silence, and the men with barbed-wire beards saw
in that creak of light that was made between
the noises of the world that was equally divided
between rich and poor, between North and South,
between white and black, between two Americas,

the fields of silent Zion in Parish Trelawny,
in Parish St. David, in Parish St. Andrew,
leaves dancing like children without any sound,
in the valley of Tryall, and the white, silent roar
of the old water wheel in the star-apple kingdom;
and the woman's face, had a smile been decipherable
in that map of parchment so rivered with wrinkles,
would have worn the same smile with which he now
cracked the day open and began his egg.